Common Language Assessment *for* English Learners

Margo Gottlieb

Solution Tree | Press

a division of

Solution Tree

555 North Morton Street
Bloomington, IN 47404
800.733.6786 (toll free) / 812.336.7700
FAX: 812.336.7790

email: info@solution-tree.com
solution-tree.com

Printed in the United States of America

15 14 13 12 11   1 2 3 4 5

Library of Congress Cataloging-in-Publication Data

Gottlieb, Margo.
  Common language assessment for English learners / Margo Gottlieb.
    p. cm.
  Includes bibliographical references and index.
  ISBN 978-1-935249-57-3 (perfect bound) -- ISBN 978-1-935249-58-0 (library edition)
  1. English language--Study and teaching--United States--Foreign speakers. 2. Language arts--Ability testing. I. Title.
  PE1128.A2G659 2012
  428.2'4071--dc23
                              2011032261

Solution Tree
Jeffrey C. Jones, CEO & President

Solution Tree Press
President: Douglas M. Rife
Publisher: Robert D. Clouse
Vice President of Production: Gretchen Knapp
Managing Production Editor: Caroline Wise
Senior Production Editor: Edward M. Levy
Proofreader: Elisabeth Abrams
Cover and Text Designer: Jenn Taylor

To a wonderful life in our new house—to the general contractor who painstakingly and meticulously coordinated every facet of construction; to all the wonderful tradespeople who dedicated their time and expertise to make our house a reality; and most importantly, to its occupants, who make living all worthwhile.

Acknowledgments

I would like to thank the inspirational professionals at Solution Tree Press who had a voice in and contributed to shaping this book, but, most importantly, had faith in me when it truly wavered! Thank you to Robb Clouse, Publisher, who had the foresight and interest in pursuing publications on English learners; to Ed Levy, Senior Production Editor, whose dedication to his craft enabled this book to become a reality and hopefully a keepsake for educators of English learners; to Gretchen Knapp, Vice President of Production, whose push for excellence resulted in a much-improved product; to Caroline Wise, Managing Production Editor, who helped to carefully rework the manuscript; and to Jenn Taylor, Cover and Text Designer, who added flair to the cover.

Solution Tree Press would like to thank the following reviewers:

Claudia Aron
Language Arts, ESOL, and Reading
 Teacher
Avalon Middle School
Orlando, Florida

Margarita Calderón
Author and Consultant
Margarita Calderón and Associates
Washington, DC

Douglas Fisher
Professor of Educational Leadership
San Diego State University
San Diego, California

Alicia Jacob
Assessment Specialist
Yakima Public Schools
Yakima, Washington

Amy King
ELL Instructional Specialist
University of Missouri-Kansas City
Professional Development Center
Kansas City, Missouri

Jan Lanier
ESL Coordinator
Tennessee Department of Education
Nashville, Tennessee

Liliana Minaya-Rowe
Professor Emerita
Neag School of Education
University of Connecticut
Storrs, Connecticut

Maritza Robles
Director, Bilingual Education
South Bend Community School
 Corporation
South Bend, Indiana

Visit **go.solution-tree.com/ELL** to download
the reproducibles in this book.

Table of Contents

Reproducible pages are in italics.

About the Author

Margo Gottlieb, PhD, is an international expert in assessment design for English learners and the creation of language development standards in preK–12 settings. She is director of assessment and evaluation for the Illinois Resource Center in Arlington Heights and lead developer for the World-Class Instructional Design and Assessment (WIDA) Consortium at the Wisconsin Center for Education Research at the University of Wisconsin-Madison. She began her career as an English as a second language and bilingual education teacher. For the past several decades, Dr. Gottlieb has consulted and provided technical assistance to governments, states, school districts, publishers, universities, and professional organizations.

Appointed by the U.S. Secretary of Education in 2008, Dr. Gottlieb has served as a member of the U.S. Department of Education inaugural National Technical Advisory Council (NTAC) and has worked with educators in American Samoa, Brazil, China, the Commonwealth of the Northern Mariana Islands, Italy, and Mexico. One of the highlights of her career was the period she spent as a Fulbright recipient serving as senior specialist in assessment and evaluation in Chile. As a visiting professor at the University of Guam, Micronesian Language Institute, she helped produce English language proficiency standards. She has been invited to present in Dubai, the United Arab Emirates, the United Kingdom, Panama, and Finland as well as throughout the United States.

Her groundbreaking bestseller *Assessing English Language Learners: Bridges from Language Proficiency to Academic Achievement* was the basis for the accompanying *A Multimedia Kit for Professional Development*. She has published an extensive array of materials, including monographs, handbooks, manuals, chapters, and articles.

Dr. Gottlieb has a PhD in public policy analysis, evaluation research, and program design; an MA in applied linguistics; and a BA in Spanish education.

To book Dr. Gottlieb for professional development, contact pd@solution-tree.com.

Foreword

The thirst for school accountability since 2001 has resulted in an overabundance of student performance data in the United States, primarily generated by standardized testing. Educators have had little say about the development or implementation of this accountability system. The expert knowledge they have of their students has largely been left out of federal policy, as classroom-based assessments are typically dismissed as informal and unsystematic. Instead, educators are increasingly being judged and evaluated by the scores that their students attain on these assessments, with failure resulting in high-stakes consequences, such as school closure and loss of federal funding. Teachers have mainly been targets rather than agents of these top-down reform efforts.

At the same time, more emergent bilingual students (also referred to as English learners) than ever before are crowding North American schools. These students are charged with the enormous task of acquiring academic language and content simultaneously within a very short period of time, lest they and the schools that serve them be penalized for failure to make required gains. Yet because the standardized tests used are typically administered in English and were not developed for emergent bilinguals from the outset, these assessments are very limited in what they can tell us accurately about the students. Thus, while more data about emergent bilinguals are now available, the inherent limitations of this information decrease the likelihood that they can improve the education these students receive.

The great significance of *Common Language Assessment for English Learners* is that it provides educators with a blueprint to develop and implement classroom-based assessments of emergent bilinguals that are closely aligned to the instruction ELs receive, yet the assessments are at least as valid and reliable as standardized tests—and likely more so, because they can offer a more meaningful picture of what these students know and are able to do. When assessments are closely aligned to instruction, it is a straightforward matter for educators to then use the results to measure the impact of their classroom practices. Thus, the data that common language assessments generate offer educators valuable information to improve teaching and learning for emergent bilinguals.

Margo Gottlieb, a national leader on the assessment of emergent bilinguals, has worked tirelessly to increase our understanding of how to accurately measure the progress these students make in their acquisition of academic language and content. This book walks educators through the development of common language assessments, pushing schools to better understand the needs of the students they serve and to collaboratively set priorities for their education. Students are engaged as participants in this process. This is a welcome turn for emergent bilinguals, who have mainly been disadvantaged by the high-stakes tests imposed on them in recent years.

What is more, this book is very important within the current context, as it carves out a space for educators' voices within reform efforts focused on accountability. One can only hope that the call from school systems across the United States for greater flexibility is heeded, and the myopic focus on standardized testing is broadened to allow for more accurate representations of student performance, through multiple measures inclusive of common language assessments.

Not only does the information provided in this book offer educators a way to meaningfully monitor their students' growth within the era of accountability, it also offers a means for teachers to reshape the directions of future policy and the ways emergent bilinguals are assessed.

Kate Menken is associate professor of linguistics at Queens College, The City University of New York and a research fellow at the Research Institute for the Study of Language in Urban Society, The City University of New York Graduate Center.

Introduction
Breaking Ground on Common Language Assessment

A successful person is one who can lay a firm foundation.

—David Brinkley

In the U.S., English learners are recognized as the fastest-growing public school population, having doubled in number in almost half the states between 1995 and 2005 (Payán & Nettles, 2008). Projections are that in the next forty years, the number of Hispanic school-age children, who represent over 75 percent of English learners, will come to exceed the number of white non-Hispanic school-age children (Fry & Gonzales, 2008). Yet when it comes to national policy, English learners are only tacitly acknowledged, and for the most part, they remain marginalized in decision-making circles.

To add to the language-learner mix, the number of two-way immersion programs has also grown tremendously in recent years. The U.S. national directory of two-way immersion programs lists a 60 percent increase in the decade ending in 2010, from 231 to 376 preK–12 two-way immersion programs scattered across 28 states and the District of Columbia (Center for Applied Linguistics, 2010). In these language-learning environments, English learners, alongside their proficient English peers, receive content and literacy instruction in English and a partner language.

Coinciding with the explosion of the language-learner population is the increase in the number of large-scale tests administered in schools. High-stakes assessment dominates the world of educational reform and has become synonymous with accountability. In the U.S., states have been required to develop and implement an aligned, standards-referenced assessment system with reliable and valid tests for all students. For English learners, both English language proficiency and achievement testing have become part of the accountability equation.

In working with states, districts, and schools in every corner of the United States and its territories, I have personally witnessed the impact of mandates on educators. The power of testing has had an undeniable effect on teaching and learning, from classroom teachers to superintendents (Shohany, 2001). For linguistically and culturally diverse students in the U.S., state-level testing, as a by-product of the reauthorization of the Elementary and Secondary Education Act in 2001, has resulted in a de facto national language policy (Menken, 2008). However, with very few exceptions, language testing other than in English has not been considered a viable option within a state's accountability system, even though two languages are the centerpiece of two-way immersion and developmental language education programs.

The resulting disconnect between instruction and assessment in these instances has forced educators to reconsider how to measure what these students know and are able to do.

Amid a U.S. top-down accountability model imposed upon states, districts, and schools by the U.S. federal government, there have been cries for assessment reform. The educational pendulum has begun to gently swing from stringent top-down accountability to acceptance of bottom-up input. The strict adherence of states, districts, and schools to federal guidelines has started to give way to local voices. As a result, local accountability systems have gradually accepted the inclusion of multiple measures, given over time, and representative of a variety of perspectives (Gottlieb, 2009; Gottlieb & Nguyen, 2007). In addition, educators increasingly rely on and use both formative and summative results to aid in their decision making. This reallocation of power and control, in conjunction with the rethinking of what constitutes academic success for students, has reawakened what we value as educators in our efforts to improve schooling. The time is ripe for professional learning teams, working collaboratively, to build common language assessment reflective of what is valued for language learners.

One of my intents in writing this book is to help teachers, school leaders, and administrators everywhere understand that, equipped with the proper instructional assessment tools, they can make a difference in the education of our youth. I hope that by offering common language assessment as a complement to commercial interim and standardized tests, educators can become energized with renewed motivation, spark, and creativity as they apply the data to their classrooms, schools, and districts.

About This Book

Accountability legislation has heightened awareness of the issues related to English learners, with an increased focus on the use of data for decision making. Schools in every state are responsible for the education of English learners, who represent approximately 10 percent of K–12 enrollment. With the increased linguistic and cultural diversity in classrooms, we see more targeted professional development, which is beginning to result in greater coordination of services for English learners (Ramsey & O'Day, 2010). Reliable and valid language data must now be collected locally on a regular basis to ensure the academic rigor of services for language learners.

Teachers, school leaders, and administrators in elementary and secondary schools need to monitor the language development of English learners on an ongoing basis. These students can indeed reach grade-level expectations based on their levels of language proficiency, and educators need to accrue a body of evidence from valid assessment of these students. There must also be local accountability for language learning other than in English. By establishing and maintaining uniformity in data collection, analysis, and interpretation through common language assessment, we get a truer portrait of these learners' language development over time. As a result, advances in the education of all language learners move from possibility to reality.

Who This Book Is For

Common Language Assessment for English Learners is intended for educators who wish to engage in a collaborative assessment project that (1) yields meaningful information for and about their students' language learning, (2) builds in student self-assessment, and (3) informs language instruction. This book is useful to teachers, school leaders, and administrators who wish to implement an innovative initiative around home-grown language data that will provide a body of reliable and valid evidence for decision making.

The focus of this book is on two groups of language learners: those for whom English is an additional language, or English learners, and secondarily, their proficient-in-English classmates who are acquiring a language other than English. In addition, although specifically geared to educators of language learners, the principles, procedures, and steps laid out here can be replicated across classrooms in almost any elementary and secondary education setting and apply to both general education and special education student populations. Language teachers are encouraged to partner with content teachers to coconstruct common language assessment tasks designed from grade-level standards and curriculum, and teacher educators and professional development consultants are encouraged to help facilitate, manage, and oversee the process.

Professional learning teams serve as the inspiration, genesis, and sounding board for common language assessment. These teams are committed to furthering student learning as they build common language assessment. Three focal questions help ground them as they collect, analyze, and use language data efficiently and effectively: (1) what is it that we want students to learn? (2) how will we know when they have learned it? and (3) what happens in our school when they don't? (DuFour, DuFour, Eaker, & Karhanek, 2004)

The Organization of This Book

Chapter 1 makes the case that common language assessment is a necessary practice in schools or districts with English learners. It offers a rationale, definition, and a framework for assessment. We invite professional learning teams of teachers and school leaders to undergo a five-phase process of building common language assessment and, in doing so, to better understand the complexity of the language of school.

Chapter 2, on the first or *planning phase*, describes the human resources required for building common language assessment. Educators' availability for and long-term commitment to a common cause—the improvement of instructional assessment practices for language learners—are critical. Planning entails solidifying the educator teams, identifying the subgroup(s) of language learners, and soliciting the stakeholders who will be involved in the process.

Chapter 3 describes the *design phase* that assists professional learning teams in sketching out the structure of common language assessment. Much preparation goes into determining the instructional assessment's purpose, selecting standards, and formulating language targets. The steps for designing common language tasks and projects also include knowing how to differentiate language for English learners and what data to collect. Finally, we devise a professional development plan to capture the collective goals of the professional learning team or district as a whole and to solidify their commitment to common language assessment.

Chapter 4, on the *refinement phase*, emphasizes the coordination of effort required in crafting and fine tuning common language assessment. At this halfway point in construction, we set aside time to review the logistics of implementation. Teachers try out the language tasks and reflect on their effectiveness, and students act as reviewers and contributors. During refinement, the collaborative teams exercise care in the selection or adaptation of rubrics and documentation forms and their match to the language tasks and projects. Toward the close of this phase, professional learning teams take time to modify the initial design.

The *inspection phase*, chapter 5, is a systematic review of what has been accomplished to date, paying special attention to the role of rubrics in interpreting student work samples and achieving reliable ratings. In this phase, we contemplate how best to communicate with different stakeholders. Most importantly, we consider using the information from common language assessment to inform instruction and monitor students' language growth with the ultimate goal of improving their achievement.

Finally, the *maintenance phase* (chapter 6) addresses issues related to the data from common language assessment. In this final building block, we take care to ensure that a viable and valid assessment system functions within the greater school, language education program, or district. In assembling a body of evidence, professional learning teams, along with school and district leaders, discuss the role of technology and formulate policies in regard to data storage, retention, and retrieval. Checks are put into place to verify that common language assessment, built around the characteristics and needs of language learners, promotes high-quality teaching and learning.

Each chapter begins with an Organizing Principle—its big idea or essential understanding, meant to spark thinking and deliberation—and a Lead Question, specifying a topic related to English learners within the chapter's theme.

Readers may find the glossary on page 157 helpful as they work through the phases of construction.

 Reproducible activities, at the end of every chapter and online at **go.solution-tree.com/ELL**, signal points at which teachers, school leaders, and professional learning teams can discuss, summarize, synthesize, and apply what has been presented and reflect on its relevance and usability in their own setting. These activities, indicated by an icon like the one shown in the margin, enable teacher-led teams to plan, implement, and evaluate every aspect of common language assessment. Taken as a whole, they chronicle the five phases of the construction process. When educators actively participate in every step of the construction process, the result is a satisfied product and an enduring system built to specification. The time has come for rethinking how to measure language learning and the attainment of language targets and benchmarks for our students and language education programs. Common language assessment can fill that niche in many schools and districts.

Chapter 1

Common Language Assessment

High achievement always takes place in the framework of high expectations.

—CHARLES F. KETTERING

Language forms the heart of instruction; thus, all teachers are language teachers (Zwiers, 2008). Since language is also a distinguishing characteristic of English learners, educators must be sensitive to students' language development. This opening chapter introduces common language assessment as a tool for measuring language embedded within instruction and, in doing so, affords teachers and school leaders opportunities to set realistic language expectations for students within grade-level, content-driven instruction. It helps explain how language impacts the performance of language learners from classroom to classroom, highlights the challenges English learners face every day in school, and offers a teacher-driven data source for decision making.

Organizing Principle: Common language assessment enables teachers and school leaders to set and measure language expectations for language learners across classrooms.

Lead Question: How does common language assessment contribute to understanding the performance of English learners in school?

We begin by looking at the adventures of a hypothetical school that set out for the first time to build team-based assessment for English learners.

Common Language Assessment at Graham School

Over the last decade, Graham School has undergone a demographic transformation, with more and more linguistic and cultural groups arriving at its doors. At the close of last year, a districtwide survey revealed that the number-one priority for teachers was professional development on classroom-based assessment practices.

As a follow-up to the survey, Graham's principal asked her staff to list the language proficiency and achievement measures that they used. It was amazing to discover that there was full coverage for academic achievement at the classroom, school, and district levels. The language educators pointed out that the majority of the measures, however, had not been developed with English learners in mind, and few, if any, measures were available in the students' native languages.

The most surprising finding was that outside of the annual state test and an interim language proficiency measure from a publisher, teachers had little instructionally based information on English learners' language development throughout the year. True, teachers collected data all the time in their individual classrooms, but collectively, there was no uniformity in assessment practices. Language teachers, in particular, felt that they did not have a voice and wanted to contribute to the school culture.

As a result, the principal decided that the school's primary goal for the upcoming year was to promote students' academic language development. One of the vehicles to document students' language growth would be team-based assessment.

Rationale for Common Language Assessment

Measuring academic language is critical for English learners, as their ultimate achievement often hinges on their use of English, a language with which they are not yet fully versed. Common language assessment allows English learners to demonstrate the extent to which they have the language requisite for accessing grade-level content. At the same time, by agreeing on how language learners can demonstrate meeting the milestones or benchmarks of language development, teachers gain a firm understanding of the complexities of language learning. Common language assessment is a potentially powerful tool and a vital component of a balanced assessment system. Adopting common language assessment practices within a grade, school, language education program, or even district is useful in:

- Informing language instruction
- Better understanding the relationship between the students' language proficiency and their academic achievement
- Offering reliable, valid, and timely language data for low-stakes decision making
- Bringing greater equity into classrooms serving English learners

The ultimate goal of instructionally bound assessment is to support learning (Black & Wiliam, 1998; Stiggins, 2008). When educators collaborate to build assessment from the ground up, they become vested in the process and advocates for their students. In this book, we examine ways in which teachers and school leaders can become contributors to school and district-level accountability through data-informed decisions based on common language assessment.

Teachers and school leaders customize common language assessment for their specific school populations; thus, the data are authentic, inspired by classroom practice, and representative of what teachers value in schooling. As a result, data from common language assessment offer:

- Credibility, with close connections to the curriculum and their related standards
- Potential instructional impact on language learning
- Value for various stakeholders, including other teachers, students, and the community

Definition of Common Language Assessment

Common language assessment is a set of mutually agreed-upon language measures or tasks, embedded in instruction, along with uniform procedures for collecting, analyzing, and interpreting data across multiple classrooms. We define common language assessment from the vantage point of teachers who, in collaboration with school leaders, set a collective vision and attainable instructional goals for their students. Common language assessment represents what teachers value, is a direct representation of what is taught, and yields useful, relevant, and meaningful information.

Common or uniform procedures associated with common language assessment include:

- Setting a mutually agreed-upon timetable for data collection
- Creating and using the **same** directions or instructions for the language tasks or projects—that is, pre-establishing directions based on the language proficiency levels of the students
- Using the **same** rubrics or scoring guides to interpret data—applying the identical scoring criteria or project descriptors, agreed upon by teachers, for interpreting student work samples or products
- Checking for reliability of scoring to ensure the **same** interpretation of student work—comparing and discussing ratings until teachers reach consensus and consistency
- Interpreting the results the **same** way—having the meaning attached to the scores carry the same understanding for all stakeholders involved, including students and teachers
- Using the information to make the **same** kinds of decisions—using the data uniformly to make informed educational decisions, such as grouping students, determining language growth, or assigning grades

Common language assessment represents the language curriculum as it is enacted by teachers and provides information useful for improving and renewing language teaching, as well as data that pinpoint how to better reach English learners and maximize their opportunities for learning. Data from common language assessment should therefore be informative and insightful into what students can accomplish given their individual characteristics. By having information available across classrooms, teachers can have substantive conversations on the effectiveness of their instructional approaches and their impact on students; in essence, they can better analyze what they teach, how they teach, and how well they teach.

Framework for Common Language Assessment

The framework for common language assessment is built on high expectations for language learners. It consists of five building blocks or phases—planning, design, refinement, inspection, and maintenance—fortified by a set of ten principles. These principles are intended for teachers and school leaders to use throughout the development process:

1. Common language assessment, grounded in classroom instruction, is a schoolwide language education program or districtwide commitment.

2. Common language assessment is an organic process led by teachers and school leaders. Endorsed and supported by administration, the initiative for building common language assessment is infused into the school culture. Likewise, the mission and vision of the school, language education program, or district are compatible with the goals of common language assessment.

3. Common language assessment provides opportunities for teachers and students to interact among themselves and with each other. In doing so, teachers and students develop a sense of how to shape, craft, and implement the process. Self-reflection and peer assessment provide student voice.

4. Common language assessment is based on a plan that accentuates what language learners can do throughout every step of the "assessment design" process.

5. Common language assessment is comprised of tasks that reflect the diverse characteristics of language learners. The tasks are not modifications of assessments developed for the general school population—unless language learners have been considered from the beginning of the assessment design process.

6. Common language assessment consists of instructionally embedded tasks that language learners have been prepared to perform.

7. Common language assessment tasks are (a) performance-based, engaging, and hands-on; (b) challenging, involving higher-order thinking; (c) connected to students' lives; and (d) differentiated by students' language proficiency levels.

8. Common language assessment has clear performance criteria that students are familiar with and know how to apply.

9. Common language assessment has minimal bias and maximum validity; its results help document students' language growth, provide feedback for instruction, assist in educational decision making, and improve teaching and learning.

10. Common language assessment has a defined purpose that matches evidence for language learning.

To what extent do potential stakeholders agree with the principles of common language assessment in your setting? Use Activity 1.1, A Rating Scale for the Principles of Common Language Assessment (in reproducible form on page 14, and online at **go.solution-tree.com/ ELL**) to survey the amount of current support for the project. Mark the degree to which you agree or disagree with each principle, and indicate how you might reword it so that it better represents the vision of your school or district.

Building Blocks

Building common language assessment involves an ongoing, multiphase cycle that specifies the information needed to improve language instruction and enhances language learners' opportunities to acquire the language necessary to negotiate grade-level content.

Note that the words and phrases used for creating common language assessment resemble those used in a construction project (see fig. 1.1). Thus, throughout, we refer to the phases as building blocks. Just as in a construction project, creating common language assessment entails a myriad of steps, decisions, and often, concessions along the way. Ultimately, however, the end product—like a sturdy building—will stand over time with proper maintenance.

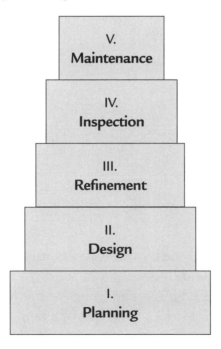

Figure 1.1: Building blocks for developing and implementing common language assessment.

For a condensed version of all the major steps in this multiphased process that you can print out and refer to along the way, see Constructing Common Language Assessment (page 16), at the end of this chapter and online.

Professional Learning Teams

Involving professional learning teams in planning common language assessment is a powerful approach to professional development within and across schools, a potent strategy for promoting school or district improvement, and a formidable change agent. By participating in a professional learning team, teachers become decision makers and leaders and transform their roles within schools (Darling-Hammond, 1996). The literature points to the following key attributes associated with winning professional learning teams:

- Supportive leadership that is actively involved in fostering, nurturing, and preserving a collaborative culture
- Members who work interdependently toward unified goals
- Collective creativity and inquiry that instill a sense of synergy among participants
- Shared values and vision that are guideposts for teaching and learning
- Supportive conditions that facilitate meeting together and encourage interaction
- Shared personal practice that fosters respect and trustworthiness
- Action orientation with documentation of results (DuFour, 2004; DuFour et al., 2004; Hord, 1997)

In addition, Robin Fogarty and Brian Pete (2009/2010) highlight seven protocols of successful professional learning teams. They are:

1. Sustained
2. Job-embedded
3. Collegial
4. Interactive
5. Integrative
6. Practical
7. Results-oriented

If professional learning teams abide by these tenets, then the isolation of teachers, especially language teachers—who tend to be divorced from the mainstream—will be converted into a coordinated effort by all educators to improve the education of language learners. Sustainability of professional learning teams requires a long-term implementation plan coupled with dedicated meeting times (for example, on early release days, during institutes, after school, or on weekend retreats) using multiple formats (for example, face to face, remote, subcommittees, or whole team) and a variety of modalities of communication (blogs, listservs, Moodle, wikis, email, and so on). At the outset, expert consultants, lead teachers, or coaches should facilitate the work of professional learning teams. As the teams mature, group members may alternate taking on the facilitating roles and responsibilities. Use Activity 1.2, Meeting Preferences for Your Professional Learning Team (page 18 and online), to help set up meeting times and a communication network.

The shared goals of a professional learning community for English learners, bound to a mission and vision of the school or district, may include:

- Creating a balanced and equitable assessment system
- Producing valid evidence of the students' language development
- Having teacher and student voices in the assessment process
- Fostering greater understanding of linguistic and cultural diversity and its impact on curriculum, instruction, and assessment

The Structure of Professional Learning Teams

Professional learning teams require organizational structures with built-in supports (Supovitz, 2002). One of the first activities of team members is to have input into determining a team's basic structure.

The composition of teams dedicated to building common language assessment for language learners should reflect the linguistic and cultural diversity of the student population within the community, the number and concentration of language groups, the types of language education programs, and the available resources. It is understood that in some states instruction in the students' home language and English is law or policy, while in other states instruction is restricted to English. Table 1.1 (page 12) shows four scenarios depicting the possible membership of professional learning teams, two at the school level and two at the district level.

Although there is no magic number, you don't want your team to be so large (more than ten) that it becomes cumbersome or unwieldy. Given the timetable, workload, and available resources, think about how productivity might be maximized. To maintain stability, it is best not to rotate members; however, it is important for professional learning teams to share their progress on a regular basis and ask others for input throughout the process.

Successful professional learning teams studying and acting on policies and practices related to language learners can be catalysts for restructuring schools for linguistic diversity. After all, the decisions confronting team members will prompt deep thinking and discussion about services for language learners and measurement of their progress. Ofeila Miramontes, Adel Nadeau, and Nancy Commins (1997) write that "schools can make a positive and significant difference for students when educators account for the complex interaction of language, culture, and context . . . [since] the most effective programs for linguistically diverse students result from a decision-making process that involves a total school community" (p. 15).

Let's take a closer look at the role of professional development in constructing common language assessment.

Table 1.1: Possible Configurations of Membership for Professional Learning Teams Building Common Language Assessment

For Schools With Dual Language Learners or Students Receiving Language Instruction or Support in Languages Other Than English	For Urban Districts With Large Numbers of Language Learners
Dual language coordinator or lead bilingual teacher Dual language or bilingual program administrator Dual language or native language teachers English as a Second Language (ESL) teachers Content teachers with English language (EL) experience Classroom teachers (preferably approved, endorsed, or certified in ESL) Assistant principal or principal	Language education program administrator Bilingual/EL special education teacher Bilingual/EL coach or lead teacher Language teachers for each grade Classroom teachers with EL experience Assistant superintendent of curriculum and instruction Local council or board of education representative
For Schools That Are Culturally and Linguistically Heterogeneous	**For Rural or Suburban Districts With Small Numbers of Language Learners**
EL coordinator or lead teacher Language education teachers Teachers knowledgeable of the students' languages and cultures Content teachers with EL experience Classroom teachers (preferably approved, endorsed, or certified in ESL) Assistant principal or principal	Director of special services Principals of schools with ELs Language education teacher(s) Classroom teachers with ELs Other certified staff working with ELs Speech and language pathologists

Professional Development for Professional Learning Teams

One of the standards of Learning Forward (formerly the National Staff Development Council) specifically addresses the necessity for adults to organize themselves into learning communities to further school and district mission and vision. The rationale behind this standard is that the most powerful form of professional development occurs in teams that meet on a regular basis. Forming professional learning teams implies a commitment to continuous improvement and engagement to advance the achievement of district and school goals for student learning.

In any cadre of teachers and school leaders, there is going to be variability of experience and expertise. The majority of classroom teachers are not well-versed in the education of English learners and the second language development process, are not cognizant of the academic language demands required for students to access content, and have not had extensive training in assessment literacy (Adger, Snow, & Christian, 2002). Therefore, it is incumbent upon administrators who oversee professional learning teams to be supportive through ongoing professional development.

High-quality, relevant professional development is one of the promising practices cited in the Council of Great City Schools' report on *Succeeding with English Language Learners* (Horwitz et al., 2009). This finding corroborates the research on the development of professional capacity in urban schools, which cites participation in strong professional development and collaborative work as key components to success (Bryk, Sebring, Allensworth, Luppescu, & Easton, 2010). Professional learning teams may be considered entities of professional development unto themselves; however, they, too, should seek additional venues for advice and expertise in order to further their own professional learning.

Part of the adventure of forming professional learning teams is the opportunity for teachers and school leaders to come together to contemplate and, at times, even debate important issues related to teaching and learning. Through conversations sparked by the activities throughout the book, educators can gain an increased awareness of effective instructional assessment practices for language learners. As a result, the group members can create a culture of trust and mutual respect, one that not only serves them as professionals but also extends to the students and the community at large. Through sustained effort, professional learning teams' commitment to the project can evolve into a school or district value.

Use Activity 1.3, A Professional Development Plan (page 19 and online), to help you plan in-service training to gain a better understanding of your language learners and fortify your common language assessment efforts.

Having established professional learning teams and ideas for professional development, let's begin the construction of common language assessment.

Activity 1.1
A Rating Scale for the Principles of Common Language Assessment

Use this activity to determine the extent to which potential stakeholders in your setting agree with the principles of common language assessment.

Principle	1 Strongly agree	2 Agree	3 Disagree	4 Strongly disagree
1. Common language assessment is a schoolwide language education program or districtwide commitment.				
2. Common language assessment is a tool for empowerment of language learners and their teachers, who collaborate and share responsibility in the learning process.				
3. Common language assessment is based on a plan that accentuates what language learners can do throughout every step of the development process.				
4. Common language assessment consists of instructionally embedded tasks that language learners have been prepared to perform, with clear criteria by which student performance is interpreted.				
5. Common language assessment attempts to minimize bias and uses results to document students' language growth, provide feedback for instruction, assist in educational decision making, and improve teaching and learning.				

6. Common language assessment consists of instructionally embedded tasks that language learners have been prepared to perform.				
7. Common language assessment tasks are (a) performance-based, engaging, and hands-on; (b) challenging, involving higher-order thinking; (c) connected to students' lives; and (d) differentiated by students' language proficiency levels.				
8. Common language assessment has clear performance criteria that students are familiar with and know how to apply.				
9. Common language assessment has minimal bias and maximum validity; its results help document students' language growth, provide feedback for instruction, assist in educational decision making, and improve teaching and learning.				
10. Common language assessment has a defined purpose that matches evidence for language learning.				

Common Language Assessment for English Learners © 2012 Solution Tree Press · solution-tree.com
Visit **go.solution-tree.com/ELL** to download this page.

Constructing Common Language Assessment

Print out this condensed version of all the major steps in this multiphased process and refer to it along the way.

Phase I: Planning

1. Pledge to actively participate in a professional learning team.

2. Identify the subgroup(s) of language learners for whom the common language assessment is to be designed, and secure statistics related to their demographics.

3. Develop a mutually agreed-upon work plan, and determine the responsibilities of each team member.

4. Notify other stakeholders of the rationale, goals, scope, and timeline for development.

5. Synchronize ongoing professional development activities with the construction of common language assessment.

Phase II: Design

1. Determine the purpose and type of language assessment.

2. Select standards to be assessed for the selected content topic or theme, and analyze their academic language demands.

3. Identify language (and content) targets reflective of your curriculum and instructional program for the subgroup(s) of English learners.

4. Suggest language tasks and documentation.

5. Create language objectives that are differentiated by the students' levels of language proficiency.

6. Embed instructional assessment supports into the language task.

7. Consider what might be used as students' evidence of language performance.

Phase III: Refinement

1. Confirm the logistical details for implementing common language assessment.

2. Review and pilot the language tasks.

3. Select, adapt, or create rubrics or documentation forms as evidence of student performance.

4. Consider input from students through self-assessment and reflection.

5. Review the assessment plan, the process, and the products; then take time to refine what's in place.

Phase IV: Inspection

1. Match language-centered rubrics to the language tasks.

2. Interpret students' work samples using the rubrics.

3. Create benchmarks as milestones for common language assessment.

4. Follow the multistep data analysis process.

5. Consider weighting results by language learners' levels of language proficiency.

6. Communicate standards-referenced results to stakeholders.

Phase V: Maintenance

1. Accrue a defensible body of evidence from common language assessment.

2. Make provision for storage of student historical, demographic, and assessment data.

3. Provide arguments for and evidence that common language assessments are reliable and valid for language learners.

4. Build inter-rater agreement of student work samples from performance assessment into ongoing professional development of teachers working with language learners.

5. Finalize and maintain a language-centered assessment system that is comprehensive, fair, valid, practical, and defensible for language learners.

Activity 1.2
Meeting Preferences for Your Professional Learning Team

What are the most logical times to meet, and how are team members to communicate between meetings? The following are some options from which to choose. You may wish to rank your selections, understanding that circumstances or policies may dictate or limit your choices.

1. Meeting Times

    _____ Before school

    _____ Common planning periods during school

    _____ After school

    _____ Professional development or institute days

    _____ Early release days

    _____ Release time during the school day

    _____ Weekend retreats

    _____ Other (specify)

2. Meeting Locations

    _____ District or administration office

    _____ Conference room in a school

    _____ Classroom in a school

    _____ Outside of school

    _____ Other

3. Communication Formats Between Meetings

    _____ Email

    _____ Blogs

    _____ Listserv or Moodle

    _____ Wikis or other electronic groups

    _____ Webinars

Activity 1.3
A Professional Development Plan

How might ongoing professional development help you produce a viable and quality project? Use the following questions to discuss the issues related to a professional development plan.

Professional development has to operate within certain financial and time constraints.

1. What internal funding sources might be available to schools and districts?

2. How might you secure an outside funding source to help defray expenses?

3. Are there creative solutions that do not necessarily require large expenditures, such as rescheduling beginning and ending times of the day, or having coaches and lead teachers in classrooms so that teachers can be released?

4. Is there any form of compensation for team members, such as being able to attend an educational conference or purchase some relevant materials?

Professional development relies on expertise for direction and guidance for the professional learning team.

1. Who might best deliver professional development to professional learning teams, schools, language education programs, or districts?

2. What school-based expertise is at hand, such as lead teachers, coaches, or mentors?

3. What local expertise is at hand, either in a district or within the community at large?

4. What national expertise may you wish to consult on the project?

Sustained professional development produces the most long-lasting results.

1. What should the format be for professional development, and how much time should be involved?

2. Should professional development occur five times, to correspond to the five phases of common instructional assessment?

3. Should professional development occur at the beginning, middle, and end of the project?

4. Should professional development be a multiday institute to kick off the project?

5. Should professional development be an optional online or hybrid course that runs concurrently with the project?

Professional development affords educators opportunities to collaborate and create a synergy that propels a project forward.

Who should participate in the professional development?

- Should it be only the professional learning team?

- Should it be the professional learning team and classroom teachers impacted by the project?

- Should it be the professional learning team and select teacher teams?

- Should it be the professional learning team and schools impacted by the project?

Common Language Assessment for English Learners © 2012 Solution Tree Press · solution-tree.com
Visit **go.solution-tree.com/ELL** to download this page.

Chapter 2

Phase I: Planning

*Teamwork is the ability to work together toward a
common vision . . . the ability to direct individual
accomplishments toward organizational objectives.
It is the fuel that allows common people
to attain uncommon results.*

—ANDREW CARNEGIE

This chapter outlines the steps for professional learning teams to build common language assessment from the ground up. It unveils the first phase of the process and poses key questions that surround the planning period. This shared experience of planning enables teachers to gain a strong understanding of the match between the students' linguistic needs and instructional expectations that are enacted through common language assessment.

We begin by looking at the adventures of a hypothetical school that sets out for the first time to build team-based assessment for English learners.

Organizing Principle: Planning common language assessment revolves around the people involved in the process.

Lead Question: How do professional learning teams determine the linguistic, cultural, and academic needs of language learners—in particular, English learners—in preparation for constructing common language assessment?

Graham School: Mrs. Soto and the Professional Learning Team

Over the last decade, Graham School has undergone a demographic transformation, with more and more linguistic and cultural groups arriving at its doors. This year, based on a needs assessment, the principal decided that the school's primary goal was to promote students' academic language development and that one of the vehicles to document students' language growth would be team-based assessment.

Formerly a primary teacher in Mexico, Mrs. Soto was excited to be a member of the professional learning team that was devoting the year to designing and implementing common language assessment. This opportunity was a first in her teaching career at Graham.

Her current second-grade classroom was composed of an eclectic mix of English learners and proficient English speakers. While many of her students were born in this midsize city, there were also some recent arrivals from Mexico, Central America, Pakistan, and China.

Mrs. Soto's professional learning team consisted of a language teacher and content teacher from each of the first, second, and third grades. In addition, there were a reading coach, a special education teacher, an assistant principal, and the district coordinator of EL services. Together, this ten-member team carved out an hour every week to construct common language assessment for the school's primary-grade students.

At their first meeting, the team formed a communication tree. The first-grade teachers set up social networks within the school. The second-grade teachers volunteered to reach out to the family members. The third-grade teachers wanted to inform the community at large. The reading coach and special education teacher served as the district liaisons. Finally, the EL coordinator and assistant principal informed the school's Parent Teacher Organization and the local school board. Their preliminary plan in place, the team felt ready to approach the challenge ahead.

Considerations for Planning

Common language assessment integrated into the school culture can lead to systemic improvement of teaching and learning. It is "classroom assessment, created and scored by classroom teachers [that] is the gold standard in educational accountability" (Reeves, 2004, p. 114). Teachers as contributors to local accountability become empowered, and with empowerment, they are able to transform educational practice. Students as part of the assessment process develop a sense of efficacy and become motivated to succeed academically (Stiggins, 2008). Stakeholders in education can become change agents and make a difference in assessment practices for English learners.

To do this, teachers and administrators must be ready to freely discuss and debate, negotiate, compromise, and advocate on behalf of language learners. Team members must be able to articulate how common language assessment provides insight into instructional practices, how the results enhance teaching and learning by providing rich and descriptive language information, and how the performance of English learners accentuates what the students can do.

Before a pencil touches a piece of paper or a computer is activated, you must decide whether common language assessment is to be implemented at a grade, school, language education program, or district level. In part, this determination depends on the size of the district; its philosophy, mission, and vision; the degree of support of district and school leadership; the feasibility of having regular district meetings; the number of language learners; and the availability of teacher reserves, such as a pool of coaches, mentors, lead teachers, retired volunteers, or even a cadre of substitutes to help in classrooms.

At first, consider developing common language assessment on a small scale. One suggestion is to have teachers engage in joint planning of a grade-level project or the adaptation of a common scoring guide specifically for English or dual language learners participating in a school-based event, such as students' oral presentations at a science fair. By starting slowly, teachers will have opportunities to explore the many options in common language assessment and to gain confidence in decision making before expanding the scope of the undertaking.

In planning common language assessment, there are many questions to pose and answer. Here are some initial issues for professional learning teams to consider:

- How is common language assessment justifiable, given all the pressures of testing and accountability in today's classrooms, schools, and districts?

- How does common language assessment fit into the district's overall school, language education program, or mission and vision?

- How, and to what extent, will common language assessment be incorporated into school or district accountability?

- What are the top priorities for common language assessment?

- How will common language assessment complement other forms of assessment?

- How is common language assessment for English learners to be weighted in relation to the other local accountability measures?

- How is the information from common language assessment going to benefit educators of language learners, and how will it benefit the students themselves?

The design and development of common language assessment require much thought and deliberation. They involve educational leaders who are willing to take responsibilities and risks for the collective good of language learners. It is often a time-consuming journey, but it is worthwhile for teachers and school leaders who band together to reach joint decisions about the education of language learners.

To prepare for the challenge ahead, use Activity 2.1, Questions for Phase I: Planning (in reproducible form on page 33, and online at **go.solution-tree.com/ELL**) to generate and document your comments, questions, or reactions for this first phase of construction of common language assessment in your setting.

Questions for Phase I: Planning

The planning phase centers on identifying all the people involved in and affected by the process. For this initial building block, we ask that districts, language education programs, or schools form professional learning teams, carefully select students, and inform other stakeholders. Here is the first set of questions related to Phase I.

Questions for Professional Learning Teams

Use these questions as a guide for putting together your professional learning teams and identifying the other stakeholders during the construction process.

A. Determining Responsibilities of Team Members

1. Who are the members of the professional learning teams?

2. Are there both language and content teachers on the teams, and what resources does each member contribute to the project?

3. Are school leaders on the team, or do they serve as coaches or advisers?

4. Does each team member make a commitment, have a role, and share responsibility for building common language assessment?

5. How might team members collaborate throughout the construction process?

B. Selecting Students, Grades, and Classrooms

1. How do you plan to select grades, language groups, and language domains for common language assessment?

2. How might you describe the subgroups of language learners? What are the students' linguistic, cultural, historical, and experiential backgrounds?

3. Do the students receive instruction in one language or two? How does this information affect the planning of common language assessment?

4. Based on available assessment data, what are the language proficiency levels of these students?

C. Informing Other Stakeholders

1. Has the school, language education program, or district leadership team been apprised of, and do they endorse, the common language assessment plan? In what ways are the professional learning teams supported?

2. Have other teachers and administrators throughout the school, language education program, or district been informed of the project?

3. Have family members been consulted or informed? Will they be involved in the process?

4. Has the school's local council or the district's board of education been informed, and has it approved the assessment plan?

5. Have the professional learning teams contemplated or explored securing outside funding for the project from community organizations or educational agencies?

In Activity 2.2, Checklist for Phase I: Planning (page 34 and online), we convert the questions for this phase of common language assessment into a checklist designed to help you monitor your progress while construction is underway.

To maximize productivity, one of the first tasks should be to devise a timeline, such as the one shown in Activity 2.3, People and Timeline for Phase I: Planning (page 35 and online), and assign charges and responsibilities to team members. This activity will assist you in setting up a calendar of events, assigning persons to ensure their completion, and organizing the building blocks or phases for common language assessment as they unfold.

It's never too early to have Plan B in hand, just in case Plan A goes awry. There may be sudden changes in administrators who want to usher in a new policy; team members may retire or change positions; even a new mandate or policy may take precedence and supplant your efforts up to that point. As a result, teams have to be solid in their commitment to and defense of common language assessment.

The Diversity of Language Learners

English learners share a bond in that they come from linguistically and culturally diverse backgrounds and are in the midst of developing an additional language. This daily exposure to and interaction in languages other than English is the major reason these students are not fully proficient in English. That said, there is a tremendous amount of variation in who these students are and how they learn. Historical background, prior educational experience, and contact with different languages and cultures make each subgroup unique.

The lives and educational experiences of English learners are important factors in building background knowledge (Marzano, 2004), contextualizing learning experiences, and predicting academic achievement. This information also helps teachers understand the starting place for instruction and assessment. Instructional assessment data, gathered throughout the school year, provide teachers with ongoing evidence to pace instruction.

Students' personal data related to schooling include:

• Language and cultural backgrounds

- Previous schooling experiences
- Continuity of schooling and amount of language education support
- Language(s) of instruction from year to year
- Affective factors such as personality and motivation
- Language exposure and usage outside of school
- Urban, suburban, or rural residence

When contemplating common language assessment, always begin by identifying the students. Some urban and suburban areas have high-density enclaves of different linguistic and cultural groups. However, in many schools and districts, there are simply not enough English learners to warrant subgroup distinction. Either way, to ensure congruence with common language assessment, teachers and school leaders should be aware of the characteristics of their English learner population. Activity 2.4, Defining the Population of Language Learners (page 36 and online), provides information that will help you gain a sense of the incredible diversity of language learners. Use this activity to start conceptualizing common language assessment for the language learners in your setting.

English learners share a pathway to full English language development; however, each is at a different point on the continuum and has a distinct language profile. Generally, English language proficiency tests report five to six levels of language proficiency for each language domain—listening, speaking, reading, and writing. This information is useful in formulating the language profiles for your English learners. Use Activity 2.5, Language Profiles for English Learners (page 38 and online), to display the distribution of language proficiency scores for your English learners.

Let's look at some sketches of English learners.

Young English Learners

The largest and most rapidly growing population of English learners is comprised of either students who have emigrated to the United States prior to entry into kindergarten or children born in the U.S. of first- or second-generation immigrants. In fact, 20 percent of preschool children (ages three and four) live with an immigrant family with at least one foreign-born parent (Hernandez, 2010). As of 2000, the proportion of English learners is highest in the early years of schooling, with these students comprising 7.4 percent of all children from pre-kindergarten to fifth graders (Capps et al., 2005).

Some of these young students acquire English, their additional language, sequentially—after they have established a foundation in their first language. Others acquire two languages simultaneously; that is, these children are exposed to and are given opportunities to learn English and another language from a very young age (Tabors, 2008). Some may reach high levels of proficiency in both languages or may be considered balanced bilinguals prior to entry into kindergarten and never bear the label *English learner.*

Fred Genesee, Johanne Paradis, and Martha Crago (2004) cite five key points from their research on bilingualism that have a profound influence on curriculum, instruction, and assessment of students from linguistically and culturally diverse backgrounds, especially during their early years of schooling.

1. There is no scientific evidence that infants' language-learning ability is limited to one language. On the contrary, research on infants with monolingual and dual language exposure indicates that infants have the innate capacity to acquire two languages without significant costs to the development of either. Simultaneous dual language children generally experience the same milestones at approximately the same age as monolingual children.

2. Children exposed to two languages from birth have two separate but interconnected linguistic systems from the outset.

3. Dominance or unbalanced development of the two languages is expected and typical of bilingual acquisition.

4. Bilingual children usually exhibit the same rates and stages of development with respect to phonology and grammar. In contrast, they typically have smaller vocabularies in each language than monolingual children of the same age who are learning the same language. When their two vocabularies are added together, however, bilingual children typically have vocabularies of an age-appropriate size.

5. Bilingual children with specific language impairment display characteristics of specific language impairment in both of their languages [and] have the capacity to become bilingual. (Genesee et al., 2004, pp. 84–87)

All young English learners who are learning English in school are by definition bilingual and are considered dual language learners.

Students With Interrupted Formal Education (SIFE)

These English learners, usually in grades four through high school, have had inconsistent schooling experiences. The designation *SIFE* applies to:

- Highly mobile English learners who might attend several schools within an academic year and, in the interim, might miss a couple of weeks of schooling
- Transient English learners who attend school for a period of time, return to their native country for a while, and then repeat the cycle
- Inconsistently schooled English learners whose language support, including the language(s) of instruction, the amount of instructional time, and qualifications of their teachers, has varied from year to year

- Refugees or newly arrived English learners who have attended school sporadically in their native country, some of whom have come here from isolated, rural communities with few schools, others who are escaping war, strife, and hardship

- Immigrants from countries with relatively low literacy rates or from areas within countries with low literacy rates

- Immigrant students whose travels throughout the academic year are dictated by parent or guardian employment in some form of temporary or seasonal agricultural-related work, including many migrant children who, by virtue of their family's transient lifestyle, are apt to fit the definition of homeless

Students with interrupted formal education often face overwhelming challenges. Like all students, these English learners are capable of eventually overcoming their educational risks. However, especially for high-school-aged students, the discontinuity in their educational backgrounds often precludes them from being able to compensate for these lapses within a four-year time span.

Newcomers

Newcomers typically are older students who have arrived in the U.S. or Canada within the previous five years with little or no prior exposure to English. Some newcomers have strong educational backgrounds; they are literate in their native language as well as other languages, and often have had advanced course work. The academic skills these students have attained in their native language readily transfer to English. This subset of English learners generally thrives academically in their new language.

Other newcomers are refugees seeking asylum from their native countries. Often, these English learners are categorized as students with interrupted formal education because of their limited school experiences. They have a weak foundation in literacy in their native language and may lack a conceptual base in mathematics and science. This group of students is faced with the dual challenge of acquiring a new language while simultaneously attempting to gain academic concepts, knowledge, and skills. Additionally, these English learners are in the midst of acclimating to the culture of school, becoming socialized with their classmates, and acculturating to a new country.

Long-Term English Learners

This subgroup of English learners has generally received more than seven years of language support, yet their English language proficiency appears to have fossilized about midpoint along the second language development continuum. Now having reached middle or high school, these students are floundering academically, generally having been in and out of various language support programs. Over the years, the discontinuity of services, often coupled with poor attendance, has produced students who are adept and conversationally fluent in English, but whose academic language and literacy remain below grade-level expectations

(Freeman, Freeman, & Mecuri, 2002). With guidance, these students are encouraged to pursue connections between school and work as a motivation to bolster their literacy and achievement.

Learners With Considerations for Special Education

English learners who struggle with school and exhibit significant difficulties in navigating grade-level curriculum, even when it is sheltered or supported, pose tremendous challenges to teachers. Many educators are perplexed as to how to distinguish language and cultural differences that are a natural part of the second language development process from a bona fide learning disability. Historically, the overidentification and overrepresentation in special education of linguistic and culturally diverse students, in particular English learners, have been attributed, in part, to inappropriate and misguided assessment, along with the preponderance of a deficit medical model. The introduction of response to intervention (RTI) holds some promise as a way to improve educational opportunities for English learners.

Heritage Language Learners

There are two major groups of heritage language learners. A large portion of heritage language learners may understand or speak a language other than English to some extent, because they come from linguistically and culturally diverse family backgrounds. Other heritage language learners represent indigenous populations who wish to study, preserve, or revitalize their minority language (Valdes, 2005). Both these groups of students have maintained their cultural heritage and identity.

These language learners can readily gain the academic language competencies to accompany their cultural traditions. Having multicultural connections and some degree of bilingualism, these students can serve as resources to their monolingual English-speaking peers.

Activity 2.6, Planning Common Language Assessment in Settings With Multiple Languages of Instruction (page 39 and online), may be useful when English learners are supported in their native language or when proficient English learners are acquiring another language. Use the activity sheet to determine the priorities of your professional learning team for developing or adapting language assessment for dual language education classrooms or for students being instructed in two languages.

Informing Stakeholders Using Data

The involvement of all stakeholders is critical in guaranteeing the success of educational programs for language learners (Freeman, Freeman, & Mecuri, 2005; Howard, Sugarman, & Christian, 2003). A representative sample of educators, such as a professional learning team, might serve as a core group. These persons are involved in planning each building block and are intimately familiar with all its many details.

Many other persons and groups, however, have an impact on the education of language learners and should be part of a circle of influence (see fig. 2.1) that helps to make decisions and disseminate information. The following is a list of stakeholders who may potentially contribute to or be informed about common language assessment for language learners:

- Students

- Family members

- Paraprofessionals

- Content and language teachers

- Support teachers (coaches, lead teachers, resource teachers)

- School leaders (principals, assistant principals, counselors)

- Language education program administrators (data coaches, assessment coordinators, directors)

- District administrators (director of support services, assistant superintendent of curriculum and instruction)

- Problem-solving teams (language specialists, speech pathologists, bilingual personnel)

- Community organizations

- Local school councils or boards of education

Figure 2.1: Spheres of influence in building common language assessment.

As common language assessment is built from the ground up, the support of local stakeholders aids in fortifying each phase and ensures the sustainability of the project. Anyone even peripherally involved in assessment and accountability of language learners should be part of the communication network. With figure 2.1 as a model, use Activity 2.7, Spheres of Influence (page 40 and online), to identify the groups that may influence the various phases of building common language assessment in your setting.

Recap of the Planning Phase

Beginning any new adventure is exhilarating, but at the same time, it can seem overwhelming. To ease the stress associated with the myriad of details, here is a summary of the major points in this first phase of building common language assessment, planning:

1. Pledge to actively participate in a professional learning team.

2. Identify the subgroup(s) of language learners for whom the common language assessment is to be designed, and secure statistics related to their demographics.

3. Develop a mutually agreed-upon work plan, and determine the responsibilities of each team member.

4. Notify other stakeholders of the rationale, goals, scope, and timeline for development.

5. Synchronize ongoing professional development activities with the construction of common language assessment.

You are bound to find this journey tremendously gratifying; all you need is confidence, courage, and commitment!

Building Blocks

In preparing to undertake this long-term construction project, the core groups that form the professional learning teams must be committed to and advocate for advancing fair and equitable assessment practices for language learners. The logistics of when and for how long the group is going to meet, how it is going to operate, and who is responsible for which activities must be all ironed out so the teams can create a synergy and run efficiently.

Teachers, school leaders, and administrators must be sensitive to the linguistic, cultural, and academic needs of students based on their educational backgrounds and histories. They need to take time to analyze available demographic, language proficiency, and achievement data to gain a firm understanding of how to best proceed in the development of common language assessment. The match of characteristics of language learners to their levels of language proficiency, academic performance, and grade-level curriculum ensures a more aligned and valid assessment.

In time, other stakeholders are brought into the fold to assist in some planning activities, affirm the direction or decisions of the team, or simply support the school or district's efforts. As the sphere of influence widens from the core professional learning team, more people become aware of or involved in the initiative. In the final analysis, a programwide, schoolwide, districtwide, or communitywide commitment to academic excellence for English learners prompts approval of the initial plan and endorsement to move forward with the design of common language assessment, the next building block.

Activity 2.1
Questions for Phase I: Planning

This activity is repeated for each building block or phase of common language assessment. Depending on the number of educators in your professional learning team, either in pairs or triads, use these and generate other questions, or raise issues to address with team members. The answers that you as a professional learning team decide on will help determine your team's approach to common language assessment for language learners.

Common Language Assessment

The Planning Phase

    A. Team Members:

    B. Students:

    C. Other Stakeholders:

Activity 2.2
Checklist for Phase I: Planning

In this activity, the questions for each phase of common language assessment presented within the chapter have been converted to commands. These statements, in turn, may serve as an ongoing checklist to help guide your professional learning team. You are welcome to convert the questions or comments you generate in Activity 2.1 (page 33) and add them to the checklist.

A. Determining Responsibilities of Team Members

☐ Select professional learning teams.

☐ Encourage language and content teachers on the team to contribute resources to the project.

☐ Consider having school leaders serve as members of the team, team coaches, or advisers.

☐ Ensure that each member of the team makes a commitment, has a role, has a voice, and shares responsibility for the project.

☐ Formulate a professional development plan.

B. Selecting Students, Grades, and Classrooms

☐ Identify the subgroups of language learners for whom the common language assessment is to be designed.

☐ Become knowledgeable about the students' linguistic, cultural, historical, and experiential backgrounds.

☐ Consider the features of the instructional program for language learners in planning common language assessment.

☐ Map out the languages of assessment and prioritize the language domains.

C. Informing Other Stakeholders

☐ Seek support of your common language assessment plan from the school, language education program, or district's leadership team.

☐ Inform teachers and school leaders throughout the language education program or district of the project.

☐ Consult with, inform, or involve family members in the development process.

☐ Inform and seek approval from the school's local council or the district's board of education of the common language assessment plan.

☐ Explore securing outside funding from community organizations or educational agencies.

Activity 2.3
People and Timeline for Phase I: Planning

It's time to start planning who is to participate in this phase of construction and how each person is going to contribute to the project. For each topic, think of the activities associated with your team, set a realistic timeline, and assign persons who will carry out the task.

The Planning Phase: Activities and Decisions	Beginning and Ending Dates	Person(s) Responsible
A. Determining Responsibilities of Team Members		
A.1		
A.2		
A.3		
A.4		
B. Selecting Students, Grades, and Classrooms		
B.1		
B.2		
B.3		
B.4		
C. Informing Other Stakeholders		
C.1		
C.2		
C.3		
C.4		

Activity 2.4
Defining the Population of Language Learners

English learners are a tremendously heterogeneous group of students. Use this activity to identify the language learners for common language assessment.

1. Review the subgroups of language learners described in this chapter, and then check against the chart on the next page. Which subgroups apply to the English learners in your school or district? Of these subgroups, are you planning to develop a common language assessment for:

   - All English learners?

   - All English learners by their levels of language proficiency?

   - A subgroup of English learners? If so, which one?

   - A combination of subgroups of English learners? If so, which ones?

2. Based on the distinct characteristics of the subgroup, combined subgroups, or the English learner population as a whole, how might you begin to plan for language assessment? Jot down some of your ideas in the column provided.

3. For each subgroup of English learners being considered for constructing common language assessment, provide some justification for the selection, discuss your preferences, and reach agreement within your professional learning team.

4. Besides English learners, are other language learners included in the construction of common language assessment? If so, which groups and why?

Subgroups of English Learners	Considerations for Common Language Assessment
Young English Learners Born in the U.S. or Canada	
English Learners Literate in Their Native Language	
Students With Interrupted Formal Education	
Newcomers to the United States	
Long-Term English Learners	
English Learners With Considerations for Special Education	
Heritage Language Learners	
English Learners in Dual Language or Two-Way Immersion Programs	

Activity 2.5
Language Profiles for English Learners

Make a tally mark or insert the student's initials for each language domain (listening, speaking, reading, and writing) and composite language domains (if applicable) in the cell that marks the student's level of English language proficiency. The language profile for a group of students will emerge from the distribution of those students. Continue your plan for common language assessment based on your analysis of language proficiency data.

Grade: _____

Level of English Language Proficiency	Level 1	Level 2	Level 3	Level 4	Level 5
Language Domain					
Listening					
Speaking					
Reading					
Writing					
Composite Language Domains					
Oral Language (Listening and Speaking)					
Literacy (Reading and Writing)					
Comprehension (Listening and Reading)					

Activity 2.6
Planning Common Language Assessment in Settings With Multiple Languages of Instruction

What are the priorities of your professional learning team in terms of selecting the group(s) of students and language(s) for assessment? Based on the results from Activity 2.5, use this chart to help determine where to begin the process, assigning a numeral to rank the priority columns in order. Then come to agreement as to which language domains and languages to use in the construction of common language assessment.

Group(s) of students: _____

Grades: _____

_____ English learners . . . any particular subgroups? _____

_____ Proficient English speakers

Planning for Common Language Assessment			
Language Domain	**Rank Order for English**	**Rank Order for Another Language**	
Listening	Priority #	Priority #	Language
Speaking	Priority #	Priority #	Language
Reading	Priority #	Priority #	Language
Writing	Priority #	Priority #	Language

Activity 2.7

Spheres of Influence

Brainstorm the different stakeholders involved in your school or district. Then, create categories for the people and organizations that will be part of the communication network for your professional learning team using the following semantic web. Use the chart to brainstorm how each stakeholder group might contribute to the process.

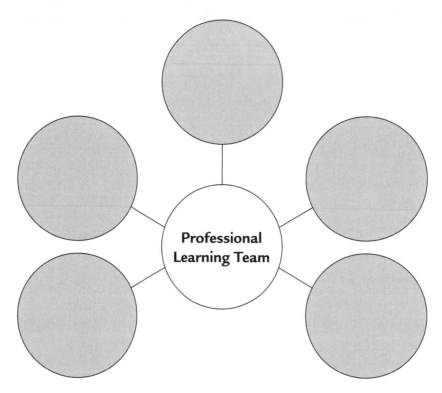

Stakeholder Group	Potential Contribution to Building Common Language Assessment

Chapter 3

Phase II: Design

Everyone is an architect of their own future.

—RUFF HEWN CLOTHING LABEL

The design phase, like the other phases of building common language assessment, entails three broad topics. The first, the overall design, focuses on spelling out the guidelines for common language assessment. That is followed by the examination and selection of standards; including the mapping of language development standards onto the academic content standards or Common Core State Standards. Finally, there is a detailed description of the components that surround the common language task.

Organizing Principle: Designing common language assessment involves the careful crafting of standards-referenced tasks.

Lead Question: What are the considerations and steps in designing common language assessment for language learners?

Questions for Phase II: Design

In Phase II, we start to put the design components together to help shape the language assessment. Guided by its purpose and selected topic or theme, we make sure that the language tasks we craft are referenced to standards.

> ### *Questions for Professional Learning Teams*
> #### A. Overall Design
>
> 1. What are the purposes of common language assessment?
>
> 2. What is the timing for common language assessment?
>
> 3. Why is academic language central to the design for common language assessment?
>
> 4. What is the framework for common language assessment?

B. Examination and Selection of Standards

1. What are your topics or themes identified from language development standards and state academic content standards or Common Core State Standards?

2. Based on your students' language profiles, what are your selected grade levels, standards, languages, and language domains?

3. What are the academic language demands required for language learners to access the selected standards?

4. How are standards referenced throughout the process of constructing common language assessment?

C. Common Language Tasks

1. How do you distinguish among language goals, language targets, and language objectives?

2. What are some ideas for language tasks and task types?

3. How do you differentiate your language tasks according to language objectives in order to reflect higher-order thinking and grade-level curriculum, even for students with beginning levels of language proficiency?

4. Which instructional supports can be integrated into the language tasks?

5. What is the evidence of student performance, and how is it going to be documented?

Using these three areas of questioning, professional learning teams facilitate the creation of the blueprint and the solid frame for common language assessment for language learners. Use Activity 3.1, Questions for Phase II: Design (in reproducible form on page 63, and online at **go.solution-tree.com/ELL**) and Activity 3.2, Checklist for Phase II (page 64 and online at **go.solution-tree. com/ELL**), to ensure that the questions for this phase are ones you wish to tackle and the items on the checklists reflect how you wish to proceed. As you move through the process, you are welcome to modify, rearrange, add, delete, or substitute items as you see fit to best meet the needs of the language learners in your school, language education program, or district.

Activity 3.3, People and Timeline for Phase II: Design (page 65 and online), asks you to identify the persons and activities associated with the design phase. Use this activity to record the assignments and schedule for the design phase or add this information onto your running file of persons and their responsibilities from chapter 2 (page 35). Don't forget to recruit an advisor, facilitator, consultant, or school leader to help facilitate the process! Once everyone has signed up, transfer the names of the team members and the assessment parameters onto the form in Activity 3.6, Organizing for Common Language Assessment (page 68 and online).

To begin, though, let's look in on how Mrs. Soto and Graham School approached the design phase.

> ### Graham School: Designing the Common Language Assessment
>
> One of the first decisions of Graham's professional learning team was to determine the purpose for common language assessment, since its choice would dictate the design. That was easy, since everyone readily agreed that the school needed valid, classroom-embedded tools for English learners in order to monitor students' progress in language development. Next, the learning team discussed the best times throughout the year to incorporate common language assessment into its curriculum. Mrs. Soto suggested that it would be helpful to have the information for quarterly reporting to family members, and everyone concurred. With built-in planning time, it seemed realistic to develop three grade-level units of instructional assessment for January, March, and May. If successful, perhaps a fourth unit could be crafted over the summer for the fall. Having made some initial decisions, the professional learning team next reviewed the activities associated with the design phase, divided up the assignments, and proposed a tentative timeframe.

Overall Design

In the design phase, we look at the purposes, timing, academic language, and framework of the common language assessment.

Purposes

Assessment serves both pedagogical and administrative purposes (McKay, 2006). Common language assessment falls in large part within the pedagogical range, although it may also serve an administrative purpose. Common language assessment may be used to:

- Screen language learners for initial placement into instructional groups

- Help in adjusting oral language development and literacy groups throughout the school year

- Inform language instruction

- Determine the extent to which language targets and language objectives have been met

- Document progress of students' listening, speaking, reading, and writing

- Monitor students' English language development in relation to grade-level language development standards

- Create a body of evidence to corroborate or refute interim, benchmark, or standardized test data, thus, providing additional perspectives for decision making

- Contribute to school, language education program, or district accountability

As consensus-driven groups, professional learning teams must agree on the purpose for their common language assessment. Having an understanding of its purpose helps establish the validity of common language assessment, and how to use the data.

Timing

When designing common language assessment, professional learning teams and the administrators who support them need to set a schedule for implementation.

As summarized in table 3.1, the purpose of the common language assessment might affect when and how frequently it occurs. A universal language screener, for example, is most likely given within the first few weeks of a new school year or whenever new English learners enter a district in order to help determine initial placement in an instructional group. If, on the other hand, the purpose for common language assessment is to monitor students' language development, then common language tasks would be given at regular intervals, say three to four times during the school year. To ascertain whether a standards-referenced language target has been met, common language assessment would correspond to the end of a unit of instruction, which most likely occurs every four to six weeks. And finally, to examine individual language skills corresponding to language objectives, common language assessment would occur lesson by lesson, most probably on a weekly basis.

Table 3.1: Matching the Purpose for Common Language Assessment to Frequency of Occurrence

Purpose for Common Language Assessment	Suggested Frequency During the School Year
1. Language screening	Once
2. Monitoring language development	Quarterly
3. Meeting language targets	Monthly
4. Meeting language objectives	Weekly

Having determined the purpose and schedule for common language assessment, we turn to one of its most important design features, academic language.

Academic Language

Academic language refers to the language that students process and use in school, especially that in content-centered classrooms. In general terms, academic language refers to thinking and literacy used across disciplines (Zwiers, 2008) to acquire new or deeper understanding of concepts, to communicate that understanding to others, and to meaningfully participate in the classroom setting (Gottlieb, Katz, & Ernst-Slavit, 2009). Figure 3.1 illustrates how social language, our everyday surface-level communication (which indeed can be academically demanding for English learners), dovetails with academic content, discipline-specific knowledge, and skills to produce academic language.

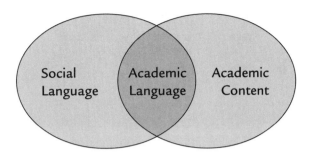

Figure 3.1: Academic language represented as the intersection of social language and academic content.

Academic language is also conceived as a wide range of language competencies related to content areas, the most prominent being the language of language arts, the language of math, the language of science, and the language of social studies (Egbert & Ernst-Slavit, 2010). Content-based academic language heavily influences opportunities for English learners to succeed in school (Goldenberg & Coleman, 2010); this more specialized or discipline-specific language should be the focus of common language assessment.

Framework

The construction of common language assessment follows a sequential process with specified steps. In the design phase, we define, describe, and discuss each component of the language assessment framework, as illustrated in figure 3.2 (page 46).

The framework for common language assessment is unique for language learners because of:

- The presence of both language and content standards
- The opportunity to analyze the language demands of the standards
- Its language (and content) targets
- The presence of language tasks, along with documentation
- Language objectives that differentiate the language task by the students' levels of language proficiency
- Instructional assessment supports
- Evidence of student performance (in more than one language)

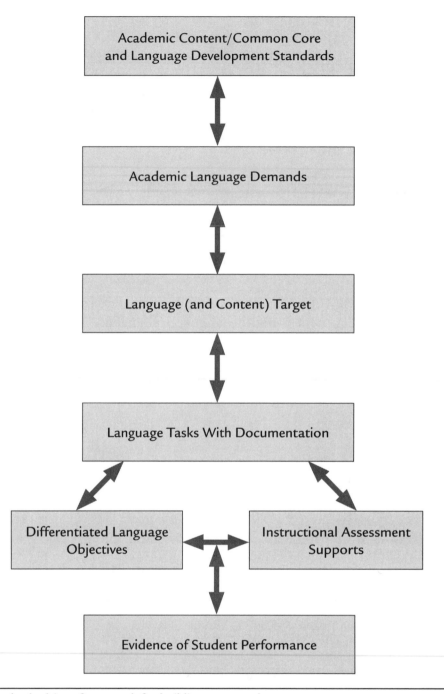

Figure 3.2: A standards-driven framework for building common language assessment.

Graham School: Designing a Math Unit

Together, Mrs. Soto and her partner generated a list of the most important second-grade math units of instruction to consider for common language assessment before selecting the topic "measurement." Coincidentally, the representation for measurement in the language development standard not only matched the topic but directly connected to the common core standards. The teachers constantly referred to the chart [fig. 3.3, page 48] in designing language assessment.

The second-grade partners chose to develop a math unit on measurement as it was interesting for their students as well as critical for their achievement. Before delving into the project, Mrs. Soto and her team partner identified the grade-level student standards with which they would be working. The state was in transition from their own academic content standards to the Common Core State Standards, so it was necessary to inspect both sets. Mrs. Soto highlighted the English language development standard that dealt with the language of measurement while her colleague identified the corresponding common core standards.

Since the standards dictated the academic language the students were to encounter in math, Mrs. Soto and her content partner analyzed the discourse, grammatical structures, and vocabulary of their second-grade math book, the supplemental computer software, some related informational books, and a content-based dictionary for young language learners. Based on the needs of their English learners, the pair focused on the productive language domain of speaking. The analysis of academic language also proved helpful in creating the content and language targets for the week-long project.

The teachers knew that providing a context for language learning offered the students the background for making meaning and motivated them to engage in learning. Therefore, they spent some time looking for informational books about how carpenters and architects around the world use measurement and measurement tools. Reading the illustrated books to the students was a great preview to the unit; in fact, one of their student's mothers was a carpenter who came to school to give a demonstration.

At this point, the professional learning team listened attentively to the language assessment expert who served as the advisor on the project. She facilitated the process of implementing the framework for common language assessment by providing exemplars for team members. Thinking about their language learners, the partners then spent a day designing language tasks, making sure that they included visual and graphic supports as well as language objectives that were differentiated by the students' levels of language proficiency. In addition, they considered how to document students' oral performance and mark evidence for learning.

Examination and Selection of Standards

An aligned instructional assessment system begins with standards that specify grade or grade-level cluster outcomes for students, teachers, administrators, and other stakeholders. Educators of language learners must be aware of the correspondence between language and content standards. We reference standards throughout the course of construction, as they are the foundational posts in building common language assessment. From formulating language and content targets, to measuring students' language proficiency, to reporting results, standards ground common language assessment.

Connection	**Common Core State Standard:** Measurement and Data 2.MD Measure and estimate lengths in standard units. 1. Measure the length of an object by selecting and using appropriate tools such as rulers, yardsticks, meter sticks, and measuring tapes; 2. Measure to determine how much longer one object is than another, expressing the length difference in terms of a standard length unit. (Common Core State Standards Initiative, 2010, p. 20)					
						Level 6 - Reaching
Example Topic	**Level 1 Entering**	**Level 2 Emerging**	**Level 3 Developing**	**Level 4 Expanding**	**Level 5 Bridging**	
Measurement Units and Tools **Topical Vocabulary** Students at all levels of English language proficiency are exposed to grade-level words and expressions, such as: measure, inches, feet, centimeters, meters, measurement tools, yardsticks	Respond to teacher-directed questions about measurement units or tools using realia. (For example, "Do you measure a wall in meters or in centimeters?")	Exchange questions and answers comparing measurement units or tools using realia with a partner. (For example, "Which tool is longer?")	Evaluate selection of measurement units or tools using realia with a partner. (For example, "A ruler is the best way to measure this long table.")	Discuss comparative uses of measurement units or tools using realia with a partner. (For example, "We should use the yardstick because it is longer than the ruler.")	Present an oral report providing reasons for selection and comparative use of measurement units and tools for a specific purpose to the class.	
	Cognitive Function: Students at all levels of English language proficiency will reason when using measurement tools.					
	Example Context for Language Use: Assuming the role of architects or carpenters, students will measure, design, and present their own model to their peers.					

Speaking

Figure 3.3: English Language Development Standards, Standard 3, The Language of Mathematics, Grade 2, 2007, 2004. From the World-Class Instructional Design and Assessment Consortium, Wisconsin Center for Education Research, University of Wisconsin, Madison. Used with permission.

> ### *Graham School: Examination and Selection of Standards*
>
> After agreeing on the measurement theme, Mrs. Soto examined the second grade language development standards and found a match to the corresponding Common Core State Standards. Figure 3.3 shows how the language of mathematics can be represented for language learners—in this case, for the language domain of speaking. It illustrates how higher-order thinking suggested by the cognitive function is present across all levels of language proficiency. In addition, as the topical vocabulary consists of grade-level words and expressions, language learners can readily interact with their peers. Finally, the context for language use suggests how students can relate what they are learning to real-life experiences.

Common Core State Standards (CCSS)

For English learners to become college and career ready, they must learn language through content rather than in isolation so that there is a meaningful context to connect ideas and concepts. To capture what students are expected to know and be able to do, professional learning teams should turn to their state content standards or the Common Core State Standards for language arts, mathematics (grades K–12), and literacy for history and social studies, science, and technical subjects (grades 6–12), the starting point for designing common language assessment.

Language Development Standards

Language proficiency or development standards express the expectations we have of language learners on their pathway toward acquiring a new language through listening, speaking, reading, and writing within a school setting. Generally in the form of descriptive statements, language development standards account for how language learners process or produce language for a given purpose within a given context (Gottlieb, in press). English language development standards have been designed for English learners who require language support to achieve academic parity with their English-proficient peers. Spanish language development standards serve as guideposts for Hispanic students receiving instruction in their home language as well as students participating in Spanish dual language programs.

To maximize their validity and utility, language development standards should serve as a springboard to and reinforcement of academic content standards. That is, English language development standards specify the language requisite for English learners to access the grade-level content identified in the Common Core State Standards or the individual state's academic content standards.

Gathering the state's academic content standards or Common Core State Standards, along with the English language proficiency or development standards, professional learning teams can match from these sets of standards to a topic or theme.

Graham School: Identifying the Language Demands

By analyzing the language in the informational books, their own math textbook, and the supplemental computer program, the second-grade pair identified the academic language demands of the unit. They realized how complex the language was, even for second graders. At the discourse level, for example, the students listened to an entire book before they realized the house being built was for a dog! There were specific grammatical structures that seemed to repeat themselves that the students had to process. There was also new vocabulary, including several words with multiple meanings, such as *ruler,* *yard,* *foot,* and *inch.* So the teachers collaborated on how to introduce the new words and expressions along with the use of real objects and measurement tools.

As they sifted through the material, the second-grade pair categorized the aspects of academic language they wished to emphasize throughout the week. Figure 3.4 shows the chart that Mrs. Soto and her partner developed with excerpts of the grade-level language their students were exposed to during the measurement unit.

Discourse Level	Sentence Level	Word/Expression Level
"Architects and carpenters design rooms—choose the one you want to be. You need special tools to measure the floors, the walls, and the furniture. A meter stick, a yardstick, and a ruler are all measurement tools. First, we are going to practice measuring. We will have partners that work together for this project."	The bookcase is shorter than the rug. The meter stick is the longest measurement tool. Which tools can you use to measure the short wall?	Architect, carpenter, ruler, yardstick, meter stick, measurement tool, measure, centimeters, inches, foot (feet), longer than, shorter than

Figure 3.4: Academic language for the measurement unit.

Having analyzed the aspects of language covered during the week, Mrs. Soto sat with her partner to create learning targets for the project. She realized that for her English learners to access the content associated with measurement tools and units, they had to use comparative language. Here were the targets the teachers jointly produced for the unit:

- **The content target**—The students will be able to measure everyday objects with standard measurement tools and report the results in standard units.

- **The language target**—English learners will use comparative language in speaking about measurement tools and units.

The next step was creating the language task to be embedded into the daily lessons throughout the week-long unit. Mrs. Soto, being the language specialist, felt responsible for this portion. Given the big idea for this theme that "Measurement tools help us design the world around us," she thought of ways to maximize use of the academic language of measurement for all students, especially her English learners.

Demands of Academic Language

Since academic language entails multiple, interrelated competencies, so too, should common language assessment. The major dimensions of academic language include oral and written passages at the discourse level, grammar or syntactic patterns at the sentence level, and general, specific, or technical vocabulary at the word and phrase level (Egbert & Ernst-Slavit, 2010; Gottlieb, Katz, & Ernst-Slavit, 2009). Inspecting the standards and resource materials, such as textbooks, the Internet, and other curricular materials, provides insight into the necessary academic language students will encounter in content learning. The following questions are a starting place to begin to deconstruct the language demands in a content-based classroom:

- What is the context for language learning? That is, what are students expected to do with the language and why?

- Which features of discourse are present in oral or written text related to this theme or topic?

- Which grammatical structures are key to processing or producing language at a sentence level?

- Which grade-level vocabulary (words, phrases, expressions) will be encountered in oral or written text?

- How will language learners be expected to cope with multiple meanings or idiomatic expressions?

Use Activity 3.4, Analyzing the Language Demands of Content Standards (page 66 and online) to deconstruct a topic's academic language demands.

Common Language Tasks

The third group of questions to ponder for Phase II consists of those concerning the common language tasks. But before we examine them in detail, let's drop in again on Mrs. Soto.

Language Goals, Targets, and Objectives

The ways teachers and school leaders approach language in the instruction of language learners varies substantially. Language goals, language targets, and language objectives all have an impact on the alignment of a standards-referenced system.

> ### *Graham School: Designing the Language Task*
>
> Mrs. Soto shared her idea with her collaborator, who enthusiastically agreed to it. The instructional assessment task for both language and content consisted of a series of measurement activities that folded into the unit. The project outcome was that the students, in assigned partners, were to construct a model of a room. Initially, students listened to informational books on carpentry and architecture and then toured the school to see different room proportions and configurations.
>
> For the language task, the students were given pictures of rooms and identified objects using comparative language. Then they experimented with different measurement tools and measurement units, again using comparative language. Lastly, the paired students designed models of an original room using the different measurement tools and units. Some of the students chose LEGOs, others preferred large blocks, still others selected Lincoln logs. When they finished, the second graders had a gallery walk and the student partners described their model and explained their process of construction.

Language Goals

Language goals are broadest in scope, representing projected language outcomes for language education programs or global curricular expectations for language learners. For example, bilingualism and biliteracy are language goals for all students in dual language education programs. Language goals might also correspond to students' self-assessment of their progress in specified language domains or their overall language development from semester to semester.

Crafting language goals for educational programs involving language learners is useful for:

- Engaging in program research and evaluation
- Broadcasting on school or school district websites
- Disseminating to other stakeholders, such as boards of education or outside agencies and organizations
- Organizing proposals to submit to different funding sources
- Evaluating summative information

Setting language goals is especially useful for individual classes or courses at the secondary level as students move toward becoming college and career ready. At the beginning of a semester or quarterly, English learners can set individual language goals, based on their levels of English language proficiency, to share with their teachers. These goals can then be reviewed in light of the evidence of language learning that students have collected over that time span.

Language Targets

Language targets are the focus of a language-centered curriculum for language learners and an ideal communication tool between language and content teachers. A language target, generally corresponding to a unit of instruction, may apply across multiple disciplines or content areas, as in Mrs. Soto's suggestion to use comparative language in a variety of contexts. This target could readily be used by multiple teachers in comparing the lengths of objects, categorizing the angles of triangles, describing the quality of water samples, or evaluating civil rights in a variety of countries.

Having language targets is useful for teachers in:

- Collaborating with other teachers working with language learners
- Preparing units of instruction or long-term projects
- Embedding language assessment into instructional planning
- Tracking students' language progress over time
- Creating standards-referenced report cards of students' language development

Common language assessment, in large part, should aim at measuring language targets for given units of instruction. First of all, language targets have broad applicability and relevance to content and language standards. Therefore, both language and content teachers have a mechanism for sharing their curricular intents. Second, language targets are generally based on academic language functions, descriptive indicators of how students use language for specific purposes. Since language targets provide a range of instructional assessment possibilities, there is latitude in deciding how the targets can best work within and across classrooms.

Language Objectives

Language objectives, generally associated with lesson planning, are the smallest of the concentric circles shown in figure 3.5 (page 54). They tend to be the most specific or discrete of the language outcomes. Differentiated by levels of language proficiency, language objectives identify the specific vocabulary or grammatical structures for students to demonstrate their language learning. An example of a language objective in a mathematics lesson in measurement for second- or third-grade classrooms at Graham School might be: Intermediate English learners will use sentences with "is longer (shorter) than," as in "the meter stick is longer than the yardstick" when measuring different objects in the room.

Language objectives should relate the communicative competencies expected of language learners for a given lesson. Language objectives help teachers in:

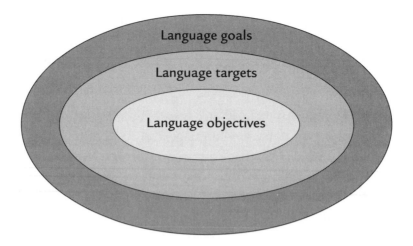

Figure 3.5: The relationship among language goals, language targets, and language objectives.

- Planning individual language lessons
- Diagnosing specific language skills of students
- Giving students pointed feedback on their language development
- Maintaining an inventory of language skills mastered by students
- Grading assignments of students

The trilogy of language goals, language targets, and language objectives is unique to the education of language learners; being able to distinguish among them helps teachers design common language assessment. Use Activity 3.5, Language Goals, Targets, or Objectives? (page 67 and online), to check your understanding of the use of these terms.

Graham School: Language Tasks

Returning to the second-grade standards related to the content and language of measurement, the language target of using comparative language within the language domain of speaking, and the specific language objectives, here are several language tasks Mrs. Soto and her collaborator considered for the students:

- Construct models of rooms based on a tour of the school and a series of statements that use comparative language.

- Given pictures of rooms, identify objects based on a series of statements that use comparative language.

- Given pictures of rooms, create models described based on a series of statements that use comparative language of different lengths of objects.

- Given a toolkit with various measurement tools, select the tools used to compare the length of objects as depicted in pictures of rooms.

Common Language Tasks With Differentiation

Having selected the standards, analyzed their language demands, and formulated the language targets for a content-based topic or theme, it's time to focus our attention on the centerpiece of the design phase, the common language task itself.

For language learners, common language assessments are designed from content-based themes connected to language and content standards. Table 3.2 offers some ways of conceptualizing how to formulate language tasks.

While table 3.2 suggests the content of language tasks, table 3.3 (page 56) shows different task types for listening and reading and for speaking and writing. Note that they are differentiated according to the students' stages of language proficiency—here we collapse the five levels of language proficiency into three—beginning, intermediate, or advanced—to create a more manageable number of differentiated groups of language learners.

Table 3.2: Ideas for Language Tasks Referenced to Language Development Standards

Social, Intercultural, and Instructional Language	Language of Language Arts	Language of Mathematics	Language of Science	Language of Social Studies
Engage in analyses of everyday actions or tasks.	Compose scenes, acts, or plays.	Make up problems from everyday situations.	Create and describe new inventions.	Produce historical documentaries.
Examine multicultural perspectives.	Produce genre-specific pieces (such as fairy tales and folktales).	Explain procedures and results of problem solving.	Experiment using language of scientific inquiry.	Reenact historical events.
Compose poems, songs, and raps.		Chart, graph, and interpret data.	Compare/ contrast stages of cycles and systems.	Characterize different time periods.
				Interpret political cartoons.
Ideas for Language Tasks Referenced Across Language Development Standards				
Make decisions from scenarios based on real and imaginary events or issues.				
Make short- and long-range predictions with related consequences.				
Engage in games and simulations.				
Research using multiple sources of technology (such as podcasts, Internet).				
Pose innovative solutions to dilemmas.				
Design and administer opinion polls and surveys.				

Table 3.3: Suggested Receptive and Productive Task Types for Language Learners at Varying Levels of Proficiency

Levels of Language Proficiency	Levels 1–2 Beginning	Level 3 Intermediate	Levels 4–5 Advanced
Listening/Reading	Match pictures, diagrams, and cartoons to phrases, sentences, or captions. Classify information. Answer yes/no and true/false statements.	Construct figures, models, or scenes. Match sentences to paragraphs. Sequence paragraphs.	Fill in cloze passages using word banks. Use technology to respond to multiple-choice questions. Categorize or order extended discourse.
Speaking/Writing	Answer questions with single words or phrases. Label pictures, diagrams, and illustrations. Make lists. Complete forms and graphic organizers, such as T-charts or tables.	Retell or summarize stories, events, and processes. Conduct interviews or student-led conferences. Produce or complete graphic organizers, such as Venn diagrams.	Provide extended constructed responses. Produce essays and reports. Create user manuals. Debate issues.

Common language tasks are embedded in instructional assessment; therefore, they represent genuine learning situations that are meaningful to teachers and students. Language tasks should be motivating, engaging, referenced to grade-level standards, and representative of the curriculum. Whenever language learners are actively demonstrating learning through the four language domains—listening, speaking, reading, and writing—they are engaged in performance-based, language assessment. While many of the characteristics of performance assessment are addressed in depth in chapter 4 (page 71), they are introduced here so teachers and school leaders can gain an understanding of what is involved in designing common language assessment. Features of performance-based assessment tasks include:

- Salience—they are meaningful and what teachers value
- Relevance—they contain real-world applicability for students
- Validity—they are realistic, with minimal bias, suitable for their given purpose and audience
- Reliability—they are capable of generating dependable data with consistency in scoring and reporting
- Robustness—they are deliberate and mindful of the depth and breadth of the language task
- Fidelity—their procedures or directions are understandable and replicable

- Documentation of evidence—they contain specified and explicit expectations, criteria, or benchmarks (Gallavan, 2009)

Common language tasks should be both rigorous and challenging; at the same time, they must be grade-level appropriate at the language learners' various levels of language proficiency. Common language tasks coupled with common documentation forms or rubrics are the essence of common language assessment. Commonly agreed-upon criteria enable teachers to interpret student performance in the same way. Assessment information that is related in terms of criteria for student success and referenced to standards is rich, valuable, and useful. (See chapter 4, page 71, for a more complete discussion of documentation.)

Differentiated Language Objectives

The language task exemplifies the chosen standards and the broad language target for all language learners. However, as we know, language learners are a tremendously diverse group of students who spread across various levels of language proficiency. Once professional learning teams reach agreement on a potential common language task, it's time to think about how that task might be differentiated by the students' language proficiency levels without loss of grade-level content rigor.

Graham School: Formulating Language Objectives

Once the language task was flushed out, the teacher team needed to differentiate the activities so that the language expectations matched the students' varying language proficiency levels. Again, Mrs. Soto, taking the lead, formulated language objectives that scaffolded from the beginning to intermediate to advanced groups of language learners. When writing the language objectives, the second-grade partners kept in mind the unit's big idea, its standards, the language target, and the language task. The two teachers were confident that this project would ultimately be a candidate for common language assessment.

The following is just a sampling of the language objectives for speaking created for the measurement task:

- **Beginning English learners, aiming at language proficiency level 2 as the benchmark**—Compare size (for example, length and width) using real-life standard measurement tools and units of measurement: "A yard is long. A meter is longer."

- **Intermediate English learners, aiming at language proficiency level 3 as the benchmark**—Compare uses of real-life measurement tools and units in various situations (for example, "I used the longest LEGOS to build my room.")

- **Advanced English learners, aiming at language proficiency level 4 as the benchmark**—Give reasons for selecting and comparing measurement tools or units in designing a model (for example, "I chose a meter as my measuring tool because Guatemala uses meters. So it is easier for me to measure.")

Differentiation of language involves matching academic language—oral or written discourse, sentence structure, and vocabulary—to language learners' levels of language proficiency. In framing language tasks for English learners, differentiation of language is a critical element, as it allows students to demonstrate their understanding of grade-level content irrespective of their levels of language proficiency.

While language development standards may recognize up to six levels of language proficiency, it is not practical to expect teachers to use such an extensive repertoire for language differentiation. Realistically, common language tasks should have differentiated language demands for two to three groups of language learners.

Professional learning teams need to be sensitive to the students' characteristics and interests. Common language assessment should reflect multiple learning styles and, to the extent feasible, include student reflection. Most important, common language assessments should invite language learners to engage in higher-order thinking.

Higher-Order Thinking Across All Levels of Language Proficiency

The vast majority of students, as language learners, have a full range of cognitive functioning. What teachers and school leaders must understand is that cognitive functions, or mental processes involved in learning, are distinct from language functions or the linguistic processes required to convey a message. Language learners should participate in tasks that entail an array of cognitive functions.

Although language and cognition are interdependent, English learners can demonstrate higher-order thinking with minimal language proficiency in English. Age is a factor; older students are more developmentally advanced and cognitively sophisticated. They have had greater worldly experience, albeit in languages and cultures other than English. But English learners do not have to have full control of the language to demonstrate their higher-order thinking. For example, with pictures or photographs, English learners at very early stages of English language development can visually analyze the characteristics of an array of animals and sort amphibians from reptiles or evaluate the characteristics of animals and name the ones best suited to their environments. Supports allow teachers to scaffold instruction so that English learners can engage in higher-order thinking; these same supports should be available to students during language assessment.

Instructional Supports

Language learners, with instructional supports, can evaluate or synthesize or reason even though they may only be able to produce chunks of language. Instructional supports are resources to assist students in constructing meaning from grade-level language and content. Sensory, graphic, and interactive supports ensure their representation in curriculum, instruction, and assessment.

With instructional supports, English learners have additional ways to process and produce language. In thinking about common language assessment, teacher representatives in professional learning teams should consider the resources typically used during instruction that can readily extend into assessment. Picture cards, diagrams, photographs, and real-life objects can be used to introduce, reinforce, and review concepts. Graphic organizers, charts, tables, and graphs offer structures for English learners to arrange information and interpret concepts. Technology, whether computers, digital recorders, interactive whiteboards, or other technological devices, affords students opportunities to interact with each other and the text.

Evidence of Performance

The last component in designing common language assessment is the evidence of student performance. Evidence can either be (1) direct, or performance-based, such as demonstrating the scientific method by conducting scientific inquiry, or (2) indirect, as in taking a multiple-choice science test on the scientific method. The question professional learning teams need to ask is "How do we know that students have met the language (and content) targets of common language assessment, and what evidence do we collect to verify our claim?"

The language task and its documentation form are the basis for students' evidence for performance; in other words, what are students expected to do to show their linguistic understanding

> ### *Graham School: Taping the Gallery Walk*
> Graham had just upgraded its technology, so it was a pleasure collecting evidence of each student's language production during the gallery walk. The flip camera was perfect for videotaping the event. In the back of their minds, the second-grade teachers thought a holistic scale might best interpret the students' language production for the unit as a whole as the English learners demonstrated how they used measurement and measurement tools to create their models. In the interim, the second-grade teachers decided to develop a speaking rating scale to use on their gallery walk; the rubric is shown in figure 3.6 (page 60). On it were the language target and language objectives for measurement. Mrs. Soto marked the extent to which each student showed consistency in using comparative language.

of the standard and how do they show it? For performance-based language tasks, use a rubric with clear language-related descriptors to document and interpret student work. In developing or adapting a rubric for common language assessment, make sure there is:

- Coverage of the important dimensions of language development (not those of content)
- Representation of the full range of students' language proficiency
- A reference to language development standards
- Well-defined criteria for assigning scores
- Wide applicability for the rubric for both common language assessment and classroom use
- Clear understanding of the language expectations for students and family members
- Potential use by students for self- or peer assessment

Speaking Protocol for Language Learners			

Rate language target and language objective based on evidence from the oral report.

Instructional Unit: _Measurement_

Date: _____

Student: _____

Grade: _____

Language Project: _Oral Report_____

Language Target	Consistently	More often than not	Infrequently
Uses comparative language to relate measurement Evidence: Language Objective:	_____	_____	_____
Levels 1–2: compares size of objects Evidence:	_____	_____	_____
Level 3: compares uses of measurement tools Evidence:	_____	_____	_____
Levels 4–5: gives reasons for selecting and comparing measurement tools Evidence:	_____	_____	_____

Figure 3.6: A standards-referenced rating scale for speaking.

- Information that helps inform instruction, yet can contribute to local accountability

Documenting and interpreting the information from common language assessment are treated in depth in chapter 5 on the inspection phase (page 97).

Standards-Referenced Recording Forms

Recording of data requires another decision in the design phase. Professional learning teams should agree upon a procedure that maximizes efficiency, consistency, and usability of the results while retaining the authenticity of the tasks. Performance-based language tasks generally rely on scoring from set protocols or rubrics. Protocols can readily be crafted from observation of students and may include checklists or tallies of frequency of occurrence.

Taking the information from this last section, check out the review steps for this phase, and put your heads together to design one or two language tasks, using the template from Activity 3.7, A Template for Designing Common Language Tasks (page 70 and online). This activity will help you continue the process of designing language tasks or start anew with another language task.

Recap of the Design Phase

How to make your architectural plans become reality is summarized in the following design steps, which have been discussed in this chapter:

1. Determine the purpose and type of language assessment.
2. Determine a schedule for common language assessment.
3. Select standards to be assessed.
4. Analyze the academic language demands of the standards.
5. Identify the language (and content) targets reflective of your curriculum and instructional program for your language learners.
6. Brainstorm language tasks and documentation forms.
7. Create language objectives that are differentiated by the students' levels of language proficiency.
8. Choose instructional supports to scaffold language for the students.
9. Determine the students' evidence of their language performance.
10. Create recording forms.

It's perfectly understandable that your initial design may not be your final product; that's why refinement is the next phase.

Building Blocks

Starting with the purpose of common language assessment, we determine the focus for the design, including a schedule for implementation, that takes the students' life experiences and cultures into account. The selected standards are the precursors to developing language targets around academic language demands that help shape the language task and its documentation form. From there, we formulate language objectives so that the task can be differentiated for the students' levels of language proficiency. Adding instructional supports enables language learners to become engaged in higher-order thinking and to maximize their opportunities to access grade-level content through language. Finally, we discover what language learners can do and document their language performance with evidence that is captured on the recording form.

Activity 3.1
Questions for Phase II: Design

In small groups, brainstorm questions you might have about the design phase regarding the three suggested topics.

A. Overall Design

B. Examination and Selection of Standards

C. Common Language Tasks

Activity 3.2
Checklist for Phase II: Design

The questions pertaining to the design phase have been converted to commands that may serve as an ongoing checklist to help direct the development of common language assessment. If you wish, adapt the questions or comments you have generated for Activity 3.1 (page 63), and add them to the checklist.

A. Overall Design

- ☐ Determine the purposes for common language assessment.
- ☐ Agree upon the timing and placement for common language assessment.
- ☐ Ensure that academic language is a component of the overall assessment design.
- ☐ Become familiar with the components of the framework of common language assessment.

B. Examination and Selection of Standards

- ☐ Use language development and academic content standards or Common Core State Standards to glean topics or themes.
- ☐ Choose grade levels, languages, standards, and language domains.
- ☐ Identify the academic language demands based on the analysis of selected standards.
- ☐ Reference standards throughout the process of constructing common language assessment.

C. Common Language Tasks

- ☐ Identify language goals (expectations for long-term proficiency), language targets (expectations for units of instruction), and the language objectives (expectations for individual lessons, differentiated by language proficiency levels).
- ☐ Check to confirm that the language tasks are engaging for students and are a valued part of curriculum and instruction for language learners.
- ☐ Make sure the language tasks reflect higher-order thinking and grade-level curriculum and are differentiated according to students' levels of language proficiency.
- ☐ Integrate instructional assessment supports into the language tasks.
- ☐ Document student performance using a recording form.

Activity 3.3
People and Timeline for Phase II: Design

For each topic, identify the activities, set a realistic timeline, and assign persons responsible for carrying them out. As there are many possibilities for each topic, this activity will help solidify the steps in designing common language assessment.

The Design Phase: Activities and Decisions	Beginning and Ending Dates	Person(s) Responsible
A. Overall Design		
A.1		
A.2		
A.3		
A.4		
B. Examination and Selection of Standards		
B.1		
B.2		
B.3		
B.4		
C. Common Language Tasks		
C.1		
C.2		
C.3		
C.4		

Activity 3.4
Analyzing the Language Demands of Content Standards

Evaluate the richness of potential standards for building common language assessment by deconstructing the academic language the students will encounter.

Grade:

Academic content standard or Common Core State Standard:

English language proficiency or development standard:

Context for language learning:

Discourse level (passages of oral or written text):

Sentence level (grammar):

Word or phrase level (vocabulary, including expressions):

Activity 3.5
Language Goals, Targets, or Objectives?

Common language assessment should center on language targets, but often it is difficult to distinguish targets from language goals and objectives. For each example, mark LG (for a language goal), LT (for a language target), or LO (for a language objective). Then check your answers with those of other members of your professional learning team.

_____ English learners will reach academic parity with their proficient English peers.

_____ English learners will use the triad "good, better, or best" and "bad, worse, or worst" to evaluate nutritional choices.

_____ English learners will improve their literacy by more than a grade per year in either L1 or L2.

_____ English learners will use transitional language in their essays and reports.

_____ English learners will follow multistep directions in response to relational phrases and sentences.

_____ English learners will participate in twenty hours of community service.

_____ English learners will convert statements to *wh-* questions to create a family member interview.

_____ English learners will use predictive language to make scientific hypotheses.

_____ English learners will use parallel language in completing a T-chart that compares the parts of an animal cell to a plant cell.

_____ English learners will maintain a digital portfolio of their major writing pieces.

Answers: 1. LG 2. LO 3. LG 4. LT 5. LT 6. LG 7. LO 8. LT 9. LO 10. LG

Common Language Assessment for English Learners © 2012 Solution Tree Press · solution-tree.com
Visit **go.solution-tree.com/ELL** to download this page.

Activity 3.6
Organizing for Common Language Assessment

Use this activity sheet to help organize for common language assessment. You may wish to create a computer file of this sheet as your ideas may change over time.

Date: _____

Tentative name for the common language assessment task or project: _____

Team members and their positions:

1. _____   _____
2. _____   _____
3. _____   _____
4. _____   _____
5. _____   _____
6. _____   _____
7. _____   _____
8. _____   _____

Advisor, facilitator, consultant, or school leader assigned to the project: _____

Needed resources, materials, and technology: _____

The Parameters for the Design of Common Language Assessment

Discuss each question as a group and check all that apply.

1. Level of implementation. The common language assessment is to be implemented in:

    ☐ Classrooms (for example, one, two, or more grades)

    ☐ Program (for example, language education)

    ☐ School(s)

    ☐ Districtwide

    ☐ Other (specify)

2. **Grades.** The common language assessment will involve students in:

    Grade(s) _____

3. **Students.** The common language assessment is designed for:
    - ☐ All English learners
    - ☐ English learners at language proficiency levels
    - ☐ English learners in a dual language education program
    - ☐ English learners with disabilities
    - ☐ Other subgroups of English learners, such as students with interrupted formal education, long-term English learners, or newcomers
    - ☐ Proficient English speakers who are heritage language learners
    - ☐ Proficient English learners in dual language or two-way immersion settings
    - ☐ Other students

4. **Language.** The common language assessment is to be in:
    - ☐ A language other than English
    - ☐ English
    - ☐ Both English and another language

    The common language assessment represents the language domains of:
    - ☐ Listening
    - ☐ Speaking
    - ☐ Reading
    - ☐ Writing

The window(s) or timeframe for common language assessment is: _____

Professional development opportunities include: _____

Topic: _____

Date(s): _____ Organizer: _____

Activity 3.7
A Template for Designing Common Language Tasks

For the given purpose, use this activity for devising your common language task or project.

1. Standards are foundational to the common language assessment task.

    Language development standard(s): _____

    Academic content standards or Common Core State Standards: _____

2. The language target describes the overall language expectations for all language learners.

3. The language task or project consists of activities and instructional supports.

4. Language objectives are derived from the language target and are differentiated by language proficiency levels.

    _____ Beginning levels of language proficiency

    _____ Intermediate levels of language proficiency

    _____ Advanced levels of language proficiency

5. Documentation or evidence of performance refers back to the language target and standards.

    _____ Beginning levels of language proficiency

    _____ Intermediate levels of language proficiency

    _____ Advanced levels of language proficiency

Chapter 4

Phase III: Refinement

Innovation never happens as planned.

—GIFFORD PINCHOT

To succeed in constructing common language assessments, team members need to claim ownership and take pride in the development process as well as the product. In addition, there should be built-in opportunities to openly engage in trial and error when implementing the plans as a precursor to revising the language tasks. These steps are all part of Phase III of construction—refinement.

Organizing Principle: Revisiting the components of common language assessment enables educators to closely examine their plans and make adjustments to ensure that the language tasks well represent language learners and that data are fair.

This chapter invites professional learning teams to put down their construction tools for a while, think about the details involved in developing common language assessments, evaluate the initial plan, and do some fine tuning. Teams should pay special attention to the use of rubrics, documentation forms, and student self-assessment to best

Lead Question: What can professional learning teams do to solidify their efforts to construct the most appropriate and useful common language assessments for language learners?

capture data from student performance. During the refinement phase, teachers and school leaders reflect on the design to ensure that it is synchronized with practice and best serves language learners. As in previous chapters, the Checklist and People and Timeline in Activities 4.1 and 4.2, respectively (in reproducible form on pages 88–89, and online at **go.solution-tree. com/ELL**), may be used to guide the ongoing development of common language assessment.

Let's check in with Mrs. Soto and Graham School.

> ### Graham School: Refining the Design
>
> Graham School's professional learning team on common language assessment had been working feverishly to complete the components of the framework. The group felt it was ready to share the process and draft products. Having outreached to other stakeholders during the planning phase, it was easy to renew contact during refinement. As was

now customary, team members reviewed the upcoming steps, selected assignments, and determined tentative completion dates.

This phase is one of reflection, so team members exchanged their draft language assessments. Using a checklist, each pair critiqued what others had produced and provided feedback. The second-grade teachers struggled with distinguishing the language target for the unit from the differentiated language objectives for each lesson; their third-grade colleagues came to their rescue. The members of the entire professional learning team then debriefed what they had learned, individually and collectively. Based on their discussions, they made some adjustments to the schedule, accommodating the block of time devoted to state assessment, but overall the learning team was pleased with how much it had accomplished.

During the design phase, some time was allocated for initial thinking on documenting student attainment of the language target, but now the options of rubrics were narrowed. Concentrating on measuring the students' speaking, Mrs. Soto and her partner decided to use a checklist coupled with tally marks for their lesson objectives and a holistic scale for the measurement project as a whole. Since they wanted their students to engage in self-assessment, the second-grade partners converted the criteria in the checklist into *I can* statements.

Piloting the draft materials was the primary responsibility of the professional learning team during this phase. When the second-grade measurement unit was piloted with third graders, time management was an issue. In addition, the immigrant newcomers to Graham struggled with measurement of inches, feet, and yards. As a result of the pilot findings, the beginners were exposed to both systems during instruction, but were accountable for use of metric measurement for assessment. Piloting the assessment materials proved insightful for the professional learning team that then enthusiastically tackled refining the language assessments.

Last year, Mrs. Soto made a rubric for student self-assessment. It included the four language domains and the five levels of language proficiency. Student self-reflection proved so successful that Mrs. Soto brought it to the professional learning team. The language target for the unit included only speaking; therefore, the two teachers pulled just those criteria and added some to make a can-do checklist for the measurement project. The students had to provide either oral or written evidence that they met the criterion. Figure 4.1 shows the chart before the teachers converted it to a speaking checklist.

Language Level	What I Can Do in English			
	Listening	**Speaking**	**Reading**	**Writing**
5	I can understand stories and reports read to me.	I can tell stories and give reports.	I can read stories and reports.	I can write stories and reports.
4	I can understand people's ideas.	I can put my ideas together when I talk.	I can read several paragraphs.	I can write several paragraphs.
3	I can understand long sentences.	I can talk using long sentences.	I can read long sentences.	I can write long sentences.
2	I can understand short sentences.	I can talk using short sentences.	I can read short sentences.	I can write short sentences.
1	I can understand words and phrases.	I can talk using words and phrases.	I can read words and phrases.	I can write words and phrases.

Figure 4.1: Can-do statements for student self-assessment.

Questions for Phase III: Refinement

Following are some questions for your own professional learning team to contemplate during the refinement phase. This is not an exhaustive list; it contains suggestions you may want to add to or modify.

> ## *Questions for Professional Learning Teams*
>
> ### A. Determining the Logistics
>
> 1. Has the schedule for developing the common language assessment been reviewed and modified since its inception?
>
> 2. What is the timeframe for administering and scoring the assessment? How is it synchronized with the general education program?

3. Has each step of the development process been clearly described, articulated, and understood by team members?

4. Is there time for professional learning teams to critically evaluate the elements of the common language tasks with the intent to refine and improve them?

5. What are the challenges, if any, of implementing the assessment plan?

B. **Piloting Common Language Tasks, Assigning Rubrics, and Involving Students**

1. Do the language tasks match the group of students for whom they are designed?

2. Do the language targets exemplify the language tasks?

3. What are the kinds of scoring guides, rubrics, or documentation forms used, and do they fit the language tasks?

4. What impact does the gradual release of responsibility for learning have on language learners' involvement in student self-assessment?

5. How might students contribute to developing the assessment, analyzing their work during self-assessment, and assisting in scoring?

C. **Reviewing and Revising the Initial Plan and Design**

1. Is the time allotted for assessment realistic, or does it need adjustment?

2. Do students understand what to do and how to do it (that is, are the directions and tasks clear)?

3. Are students motivated and engaged in the language tasks?

4. Are there differentiated language objectives and instructional supports for the language tasks?

5. Does the rubric or scoring guide capture the standards-referenced criteria represented in the performance tasks?

6. How might evidence for language learning be recorded?

     Take some of that protected time you have together as a learning team and decide who should be assigned to the suggested activities in Activity 4.3, People and Timeline for Phase III: Refinement (page 90 and online).

Determining the Logistics

This is the time in the development process to step back, contemplate the decisions made to date, and regroup, if necessary, to enhance the viability of common language assessment. At this point, consensus by the professional learning team revolves around the logistics related to piloting or trying out the common language tasks. The trial period increases the likelihood that the final assessment will be a reliable and valid index of the performance of language learners.

Schools are dynamic institutions that are forever changing due to internal and external influences. As a result, there are unforeseen circumstances and unexpected delays, so what originally may have been considered the ideal timeframe for construction may no longer be realistic. Now is the time to take stock of the schedule, make the necessary adjustments, and communicate the status of the project to stakeholders.

In a similar vein, professional learning teams should ask themselves whether they are still in agreement with the original timetable for giving and scoring common language assessments. Perhaps common language assessment has not yet been coordinated with the district's effort to create common content assessment. Perhaps the teams have been overly ambitious in their initial estimation of how much they could accomplish; it might be more realistic to collect data on a quarterly rather than monthly basis, for example. Decisions should be made regarding the specific window in which the common language assessments are to be given and when scoring should occur, followed by securing the dates on the school or district calendar.

As part of refinement, teams should step back to critically analyze the design elements with an eye toward:

- Standardization or uniformity of the directions for the language task
- Clarity and comprehensibility of directions for students
- Format or presentation of the materials related to the task
- Representation of academic language associated with grade-level curriculum
- The value and relevance of the language target
- The rigor of the language task and the match with its documentation form
- Differentiation of language objectives by language proficiency levels
- Relevance of instructional assessment supports, such as illustrations or graphics
- Evidence of language learning

Professional learning teams have to anticipate the challenges to completing construction in a timely fashion, such as disagreement on what is to be measured, how it is to be measured, how results are to be reported, and how those results will contribute to local accountability. Now is the time to resolve these issues. Above all, during this process, educator teams must remain advocates for language learners.

Piloting Common Language Tasks

As with more high-stakes tests, pilot testing the materials with students will help determine the appropriateness and usefulness of the common language tasks. It might be advisable to try out the language tasks with teachers who know the individual or small groups of students well. These teachers will be excellent judges of whether the language tasks are representative of the selected standards and related language targets. In addition, because teachers will ultimately implement the common language assessment plan, they are in the best position to provide feedback to the professional learning teams.

Optimally, common language tasks are performance-based, requiring students to actively engage in demonstrating what they know and are able to do in creative and original ways. According to Robert Linn, Eva Baker, and Stephen Dunbar (1991), validation of complex performance assessment is contingent on the following:

- Evidence of outcomes
- Fairness
- Higher-order thinking
- Meaningfulness
- Quality of content
- Comprehensiveness of coverage
- Justifiable cost

In addition to these attributes, some aspects of common language tasks are unique to language learners, including:

- The match between the selected language standards and language target
- Appropriateness of the task for the age, grade, and experiences of students
- High expectations for English learners for their given levels of language proficiency
- Students' language(s) of instruction
- The potential presence of linguistic, cultural, socioeconomic, or gender bias

Another sign of validity in assessment, as in curriculum, is the correspondence among the standards, language tasks, and language targets. This is the time to check whether these components of the design directly correlate. Use Activity 4.4, Questions for Review Prior to Piloting Common Language Assessment Tasks (page 91 and online), to review and modify your common language assessment plan and language tasks.

The purpose of the pilot is to test out the language tasks, not the language learners. Activity 4.5, Pilot and Feedback From a Common Language Assessment Task (page 93 and online), may help you decide how to approach the trial run. Students for whom the common language assessment is designed should not take part in the pilot, because it could create a practice effect that might inflate future results. Also, for the pilot, professional learning teams should:

- Recruit resource teachers, lead teachers, or coaches
- Select a small group, perhaps around five language learners above and below the task's language proficiency levels, as well as a few students proficient in English or the students' native language (if the language tasks are in a language other than English)
- Provide clear directions of the expectations for teachers in regard to information gathering
- Set aside a time to meet with teachers before and after the pilot

Before the trial period, gather all the educators who are to participate in the pilot and:

- Review the purpose and value of developing common language assessment tasks
- Provide a synopsis of the construction process to date
- Discuss procedures regarding the administration of the common language tasks
- Decide on the information to be collected on the review form to provide feedback on the language assessment (Activity 4.5)
- Provide an opportunity to debrief and make recommendations post pilot

In most instances, the common language tasks will be performance-based; therefore, performance criteria are necessary to judge the quality of the responses. Irrespective of their levels of language proficiency, students should be aware of the criteria by which their work is to be interpreted. One way to communicate language expectations to students is to introduce rubrics and other types of documentation early in the instructional assessment cycle.

Assigning Rubrics

Rubrics are scoring templates that allow stakeholders to interpret student performance in a uniform way. When developed by learning teams through consensus, rubrics provide a means of codifying what is important to teaching and learning and establishing a strong connection between instruction and assessment. Therefore, rubrics hold great promise for use with common language assessment.

Rubrics created or modified for language learners, in particular English learners, need to account for the unique set of characteristics of this group of students, as follows:

- The progression of second language development—the scaffolding of expectations of students' processing and production of language across levels of language proficiency
- The students' levels of oral proficiency in English (or their other language)—the extent to which academic language affects oral communication in content-area classrooms
- The students' levels of literacy in English (or their other language)—the extent to which reading and writing affect students' access to content

- The influence of English learners' home language in their English language development—the positive (and negative) transfer of concepts, skills, and cognates from one language to another

- The presence of cultural or sociocultural nuances—how students' life experiences, socioeconomic status, and cultural traditions influence their performance in school

- The students' familiarity with performance assessment and the criteria of rubrics—opportunities for students to engage in higher-order thinking and challenging tasks that are tied to specific descriptors to interpret work samples

An important first step is to design, adapt, or select rubrics that capture the language targets derived from state standards or Common Core State Standards. The next step is to match the type of rubric to the common language task. From there, score or analyze the information, report the results for decision making, and provide feedback to students.

Types of Rubrics for Interpreting Student Performance

Generally, there are four different kinds of rubrics: checklists, rating scales, holistic scales, and analytic scales. Within these categories, there are two variations: a general rubric with criteria applicable to multiple tasks and a task-specific rubric that is crafted for particular tasks or projects (Ainsworth & Viegut, 2006; Gottlieb, 2006). Table 4.1 describes the types of general rubrics and gives an example of their use in the context of language learning.

Table 4.1: Types of Rubrics and Their Potential Uses for Common Language Assessment

Type of Rubric	Description	Example of Use
Checklists	Dichotomous scales (with only two options): traits, skills, strategies, or behaviors are either present or absent.	A self-check for students to use before or after the many steps in producing process writing pieces
Rating Scales	Numerical scales: defining traits, skills, strategies, or behaviors incrementally by their quality (how well) or their frequency (how often)	A language-use survey that addresses the various settings in which students or families use different languages
Holistic Scales	Developmental scales (from lowest to highest or vice versa): each level of performance describes overall student competencies.	A summary of students' performance in an oral dramatization or re-enactment
Analytic Scales	Developmental scales (from lowest to highest or vice versa), generally presented as matrices: dimensions or traits and levels of performance define a competence, such as writing.	A rating of each dimension of a language portfolio to create a student profile

Source: Adapted from The Language Proficiency Handbook: A Practitioner's Guide to Instructional Assessment *(1999), by Margo M. Gottlieb. Springfield, Illinois: State Board of Education.*

Rubrics identify the criteria for interpreting common language assessment. With language tasks, these criteria focus on the defining features of language proficiency. While checklists and rating scales are useful for capturing activities or short-term language tasks, holistic and analytic scales offer a means of documenting more in-depth, long-term tasks and projects. Figure 4.2 (page 80) is an example of a five-point holistic scale for listening comprehension, while figure 4.3 (page 81) takes the identical criteria and converts them into dimensions of an analytic scale. Whoever ultimately scores the common language tasks should have input into which rubric would be most appropriate and yield information that would help inform instruction.

Some types of documentation may be generated by the students themselves as part of the assessment. For example, students' self-reflection during and at the culmination of a unit of study allows time for them to process and critique their own language learning. Table 4.2 lists types of documentation, other than rubrics, along with their descriptions, examples, and potential usability by students and/or teachers. Although information from all these documentation forms may not be amenable for aggregating across classrooms to build common language assessment, it does help personalize communication among students, teachers, and family members.

Table 4.2: Types of Documentation, Other Than Rubrics, for Use by Teachers and Students

Type of Documentation	Description	Example of Use	By Students	By Teachers
Tallies	Number of occurrences of specified behaviors or skills	Use of a specified language frame or pattern	X	X
Structured Narratives	Written or descriptive oral feedback of student work	Alternative or supplement to grades		X
Project Descriptors	Criteria of expectations or success for long-term products	Student self-monitoring and assessment of projects	X	X
Language Logs	Written account of language learned over time in content classes	Explanations or examples of language targets or language objectives	X	
Interactive Journals	Open communiqué between teachers and students that shows growth in experiential writing over time	Ice breakers or language challenges at the beginning of the school day or class period	X	X

Language Proficiency Level	Listening Criteria Overall, the language learner, when listening:
Level 5	Applies abstract concepts to show implicit oral comprehension
	Comprehends extended oral discourse with embedded multiple meaning(s), sarcasm, or nuances
	Uses listening comprehension strategies similar to proficiently speaking peers
	Exhibits receptive vocabulary comparable to proficient English peers
	Fully understands what is said in social and academic settings
Level 4	Comprehends explicit and some implicit oral language
	Focuses on extended oral discourse with some embedded multiple meanings
	Uses listening comprehension strategies with little reliance on contextual clues
	Expands receptive vocabulary to include specific and some technical words and expressions
	Understands oral language in social and most academic settings with instructional supports
Level 3	Follows multistep oral directions and comprehends explicit oral language
	Focuses on multiple sentences as the gist of utterances
	Uses listening comprehension strategies involving key words, expressions, and short sentences with instructional supports
	Increases lexicon, maintaining a larger receptive than productive vocabulary
	Understands oral language in social and most academic settings with instructional supports
Level 2	Follows explicit oral directions
	Focuses on key words, expressions, and short utterances
	Continues to develop listening comprehension strategies with instructional supports
	Continues to develop general receptive vocabulary
	Continues to gain understanding of what is said with instructional supports
Level 1	Follows simple, explicit oral directions when modeled
	Focuses on modeled key words and expressions
	Begins to develop listening comprehension strategies through modeling
	Begins to associate sound with meaning to build a receptive vocabulary
	Begins to understand what is said, often with repetition, gestures, and other instructional supports

Figure 4.2: A sample holistic scale to measure listening comprehension of language learners.

Language Proficiency Level	Dimensions of Listening Comprehension				
	Explicit and Implicit Comprehension	Discourse in Comprehension	Listening Comprehension Strategies	Receptive Vocabulary	Comprehension in Social and Academic Settings
Level 5	Applies abstract concepts to show implicit oral comprehension	Comprehends extended oral discourse with embedded multiple meaning(s), sarcasm, or nuances	Uses listening comprehension strategies similar to proficiently speaking peers	Exhibits receptive vocabulary comparable to proficient English peers	Fully understands what is said in social and academic settings
Level 4	Comprehends explicit and some implicit oral language	Focuses on extended oral discourse with some embedded multiple meanings	Uses listening comprehension strategies with little reliance on contextual clues	Expands receptive vocabulary to include specific and some technical words and expressions	Understands oral language in social and most academic settings with instructional supports
Level 3	Follows multistep oral directions and comprehends explicit oral language	Focuses on multiple sentences as the gist of utterances	Uses listening comprehension strategies involving key words, expressions, and short sentences with instructional supports	Increases lexicon, maintaining a larger receptive vocabulary to include specific words and expressions	Understands oral language in social and most academic settings with instructional supports
Level 2	Follows explicit oral directions	Focuses on key words, expressions, and short utterances	Continues to develop listening comprehension strategies with instructional supports	Continues to develop general receptive vocabulary	Continues to gain understanding of what is said with instructional supports
Level 1	Follows simple, explicit oral directions when modeled	Focuses on modeled key words and expressions	Begins to develop listening comprehension strategies through modeling	Begins to associate sound with meaning to build a receptive vocabulary	Begins to understand what is said, often with repetition, gestures, and other instructional supports

Figure 4.3: A sample analytic scale to measure listening comprehension of language learners.

With so many rubrics and types of documentation, it's time to decide which ones are most appropriate for your common language tasks. One tip for selecting, modifying, or developing rubrics is that, to yield useful information, they need to match the purpose of the assessment. Using Activity 4.6, Selecting Types of Rubrics and Documentation (page 94 and online), either individually, with other teachers, or in professional learning teams, think about common language tasks that have been designed for your grade, language education program, or school. Then use the list in the activity as a reference, and match each task to a corresponding rubric or type of documentation. When you finish, share your findings and come to agreement as to the most appropriate form of documentation for the common language tasks.

Gradual Release of Responsibility to Language Learners

The older the students, the more they need to assume personal accountability for learning. It is important, especially for English learners who may not know or understand the socio-cultural ways of U.S. or Canadian schools, that teachers gradually release responsibility for language learning to them. The premise behind this instructional framework is that there is an acknowledged transition from teacher knowledge to student understanding. Nancy Frey and Doug Fisher (2006) identify four phases according to which students become independent learners; they have been adapted here for use with English learners:

1. **Focus lessons,** in which teachers model their own metacognitive processes to establish the purpose of the lesson and share language (and content) objectives as well as criteria for success with the students

2. **Guided instruction,** in which teachers facilitate or lead students through model tasks to increase English learners' understanding of language

3. **Collaborative learning,** in which students have opportunities to consolidate their understanding of language by exploring ways to problem solve, discuss, negotiate, and debate with their peers in interactive ways

4. **Independent learning,** when students practice applying information and knowledge related to language to new situations and engage in self- or peer assessment

In this transformative teaching framework, teachers first model, then students practice, and finally, teachers provide feedback as a precursor for students working independently. These phases can be directly applied to designing and refining common language assessment.

Involving Students

Using the premises behind the gradual release of responsibility, introduce students to common language assessment. There are a variety of ways for teachers to involve language learners from the onset and maintain their engagement throughout the process. Here are some ideas:

- Given a topic, theme, or big idea, brainstorm ideas for common language tasks and projects with the students. As teachers gather information on students' interests, they are also assessing their students' background knowledge on the topic. Ultimately, the project that evolves from this discussion is meaningful for the students. During this time, teachers can note, using tallies for example, the language features that are most challenging for the students and think of how they may later be converted into language targets.

- Make sure the language tasks rely on a variety of language domains and utilize an array of technologies to allow for differentiation of language (for example, creating and narrating a video; re-enacting literature or an historical event; listening to a podcast). As a whole group, list students' suggestions on an overhead projector, computer, whiteboard, or SMART board, or have cooperative groups of students generate their own ideas.

- Depending on their levels of language proficiency, offer each group of students a set of options for common language tasks and projects from the master list. Explain what might be expected in the common language assessment, and then have students prioritize their choices.

- Share with the students the features of common language assessment. Prepare students for the possibility that their group's selection may ultimately not be the one that is used, but that their ideas are always valued. Develop some of the students' suggestions into in-class activities.

- Use think-alouds as part of the development process; give students opportunities to react to aspects of the language task, including directions, format, illustrations, graphics, content, pace, and time on task. In other words, invite language learners to try out parts of the language task and give feedback in their native language (if shared by a number of students) or English.

- Depending on the classrooms and their familiarity with rubrics or scoring guides, ask students to help formulate guidelines for scoring based on standards, language targets, and standards-referenced criteria that are used to measure language.

Think about how you might apply these ideas to your setting, using Activity 4.7, Involving Students in Instructional Assessment (page 95 and online), to help you define the role of students in constructing language assessment.

Alison Bailey and Margaret Heritage (2008) name two related aspects integral to formative assessment that also pertain to common language assessment: student involvement and feedback. Student engagement in assessment involves peer and self-reflection that enable students to have some control over their learning. By being active participants, students become aware of the criteria that constitute success and, with the guidance of teachers, can identify the next steps in their learning.

Common language assessment may be used on a formative basis, since it has a feedback loop to teachers and students. Feedback to students involves giving them opportunities to reflect on their learning. Student feedback may be:

- Standards-referenced, when students compare their performance against criteria (of the language development standard) or language target being measured

- Reflective, when students personally respond to the instructional assessment, such as relating what they have learned or what has influenced their learning
- A combination of the two (Gottlieb, 2006)

In constructing the language tasks, consider including student self-reflection either at the completion of a task or project or throughout the construction process. Students, under the guidance of teachers, may gradually become critics of their own work. The following suggestions illustrate how language learners, like all students, can become aware of how their work is evaluated and become active participants in assessment.

English learners can evaluate the extent to which they feel that they have met the standards and language target addressed in the task or project using a rating scale from 1 (still missing it) to 4 (hit the mark). With modeling, they can add evidence directly from their work samples to justify their choices on the rubric. Finally, students can react to how they think their work meets the language target for the unit or the language objectives for individual lessons. This information can be presented orally or in writing and in the students' first or second language.

Students have the right to know the criteria by which their work is interpreted, whether the work is a daily in-class assignment or common language assessment administered on a quarterly basis. Using the ideas we have presented on involving students, here are some ideas for furthering the involvement of students in the assessment process.

While students are not part of scoring common language tasks, it is important that they understand the scoring criteria present in the rubric and have opportunities to use the criteria in self- or peer assessment. As part of instruction, classroom teachers can introduce each criterion individually and then have students practice interpreting their own work against models of student samples. Once the students are comfortable with one criterion, add another over the course of several weeks until all criteria of a rubric are thoroughly familiar to them.

For instance, if an analytic scale is used for common language assessment, concentrate on presenting the criteria one dimension at a time. Keeping these tips in mind, teachers should:

- Define the terms describing the criteria with illustrated examples—if feasible, have students translate the criteria to create rubrics or documentation forms in multiple languages
- Practice using the vocabulary descriptive of the criteria in oral (and written) feedback to the students
- Score anonymous student samples on an overhead, whiteboard, or SMART board using specified criteria
- In pairs or partners, have students exchange information about their work incorporating the vocabulary terms and expressions
- Encourage students to self-assess using the vocabulary in the rubric and ask them to show evidence of the presence of the stated criteria for each dimension
- Extend self-assessment to peer assessment, in which students have opportunities to interact and defend their selection of criteria

By sharing criteria for measuring standards-referenced language targets, English learners get a clearer picture of performance expectations and lose some of the fear and mystery of assessment. Student work samples, when scored as a whole class and small groups, equip students with strategies of how to engage in self- and peer assessment.

Following the tips presented earlier (see fig. 4.1, page 73, for example), teachers or learning teams might consider converting the criteria for common language assessment into student-friendly terms. Although rubrics or other forms for student self-assessment should be introduced one at a time, once students have become acclimated, they can be guided to examine their own language development. In addition, the rubrics, along with the student samples, are useful in conducting student-led conferences.

Activity 4.7, Sharing Instructional Assessment Criteria With Students (page 95 and online), invites teachers or professional learning teams to transform a rubric designed for use with language learners into a rubric for student self-assessment. Use this time to help craft student-centered criteria to be used for student self- or peer assessment.

In the final section of the chapter, we revisit the initial assessment plan.

Reviewing and Revising the Initial Plan and Design

Based on stakeholder experiences to date, here are some questions to ask those involved in the initial language assessment plan and design. Modifications should then be made based on the responses.

- Have all members of the professional learning teams actively participated, and have their efforts solidified during the construction process? In other words, is there synergy in the group that can carry and sustain the effort of implementing common language assessment?
- Is the work plan being carried out according to schedule, and have all team members contributed to the project? Have additional activities or steps been identified along the way, and if so, has time been allocated to extending the project?
- How have other stakeholders, including school boards, administrators, family members, and students, reacted to the plan, and has their feedback been incorporated into its revision?

Information collected from the language tasks piloted with students provides some insight into the logistics of administration and their relevance to English learners.

- Is there a clear connection among curriculum, instruction, and assessment?
- Based on information from the pilot, are the language tasks appropriate and meaningful for the language learners for whom the assessment has been designed?
- Is the time allocated for the common language assessment, including gathering resources, giving directions, doing the language task, and scoring, reasonable?

Finally, in examining the language tasks, here is the last set of useful questions as we move into the final phases of building common language assessment.

- Are the directions for giving the common language tasks clear and understandable for all students; that is, do all students start on an equal footing, given their level of language proficiency?

- Do the language tasks take the students' background knowledge into account so that bias is minimized?

- Do the language tasks engage the students?

- Are the students aware of the overall language target and the specific language objectives they are to meet?

- Are the students given needed instructional supports, such as visuals, to accomplish the language task?

- Do the students know the evidence they are to produce, and are they familiar with the criteria by which their work will be interpreted?

Recap of the Refinement Phase

The refinement phase marks the midway point in building common language assessments. Professional learning teams now have a firm sense of what is entailed in constructing and implementing language tasks. As a recap, here, in abbreviated form, are the steps to be undertaken:

1. Confirm the logistical details in implementing common language assessment.
2. Review and pilot the language tasks.
3. Select, adapt, or create rubrics or documentation forms as evidence of student performance.
4. Consider input from students through self-assessment and reflection.
5. Review the assessment plan, the process, and the products; then take time to refine what's in place.

Building Blocks

During the refinement phase, professional learning teams roll up their sleeves and become immersed in building common language assessments. Every facet of construction, from the initial plan to the design, is scrutinized and checked for efficacy, appropriateness, and usefulness for language learners.

During this phase, stakeholders have been apprised of the progress of the project and have had a voice in fine tuning some of the rough edges. Efforts have been redoubled to synchronize schedules, prepare the common language tasks, match the tasks to rubrics, and collect information from the pilot. Language learners offer suggestions along the way for improving the tasks, give feedback during the pilot, and engage in self-assessment.

So, here is the last, but most important question of this chapter. After all the work to date, are there viable language tasks that can be adopted for common language assessment?

During the inspection phase, we analyze both quantitative and qualitative data gathered during refinement to aid in making decisions.

Activity 4.1
Questions for Phase III: Refinement

Jot down comments or ideas to help guide your thinking during the refinement phase of construction.

A. Determining the Logistics

B. Piloting Common Language Tasks, Assigning Rubrics, and Involving Students

C. Reviewing and Revising the Initial Plan and Design

Activity 4.2
Checklist for Phase III: Refinement

Modify this checklist based on your discussion of the topics related to the refinement phase of construction in Activity 4.1 (page 88).

A. Determining the Logistics

☐ Review and adjust the schedule for developing the common language assessment.

☐ Set and synchronize the timeframe for administering and scoring the common language assessment so that it is synchronized with that of the general education program.

☐ Describe each step of the development process so that it is understood by all members of the team.

☐ Allocate time to evaluate the tasks with the intent to refine or improve them.

☐ Identify challenges in implementing common language assessment.

B. Piloting Common Language Tasks, Assigning Rubrics, and Involving Students

☐ Determine if there is a match of the common language tasks to the group of students for which they are designed.

☐ Check that the language targets exemplify the language tasks.

☐ Scaffold instruction so that there is a gradual release of responsibility for learning for English learners to allow for student self-assessment.

☐ Use scoring guides, rubrics, or documentation forms to fit the common language tasks and gather evidence of student performance.

☐ Involve students in developing common language assessment, analyzing their work during self-assessment, and scoring.

C. Reviewing and Revising the Initial Plan and Design

☐ Set a realistic timeframe for implementing common language assessment based on feedback from stakeholders.

☐ Make sure students understand what to do and how to do it.

☐ Check to see that students are motivated and engaged in the language tasks.

☐ Present standards-referenced criteria in a rubric or scoring guide that represents the performance tasks.

☐ Inform students of the evidence they are to produce and familiarize them with the criteria by which their work will be interpreted.

Activity 4.3
People and Timeline for Phase III: Refinement

Brainstorm activities associated with the refinement phase of construction, set a realistic timeline, and assign persons responsible for carrying them out.

The Refinement Phase: Activities and Decisions	Beginning and Ending Dates	Person(s) Responsible
A. Determining the Logistics		
A.1		
A.2		
A.3		
A.4		
B. Piloting Common Language Tasks, Assigning Rubrics, and Involving Students		
B.1		
B.2		
B.3		
B.4		
C. Reviewing and Revising the Initial Plan and Design		
C.1		
C.2		
C.3		
C.4		

Activity 4.4
Questions for Review Prior to Piloting Common Language Assessment Tasks

Use this review form to analyze your language assessment plan and common language tasks. Highlight those items that may need some work, and think about how you might make modifications.

Is the language assessment plan:

1. Agreed upon by the professional learning team?

2. Accepted by other stakeholders, including resource and classroom teachers?

3. Supported by the school and district administration?

4. Comprehensive, including a descriptive feedback loop for students and teacher reflection?

If necessary, how might you modify the plan?

Are the common language tasks:

1. Standards-referenced?

2. Representative of the language target?

3. Appropriate for the age, grade, or experiences of the students?

4. Reflective of the language learners' levels of language proficiency?

5. Considerate of the students' background knowledge?

6. Matched to the students' language(s) of instruction?

7. Relatively free of linguistic, cultural, socioeconomic, age, or gender bias?

Common Language Assessment for English Learners © 2012 Solution Tree Press · solution-tree.com
Visit **go.solution-tree.com/ELL** to download this page.

8. Given within a sensible timeframe?

9. A realistic portrayal of what language learners can do?

If necessary, how might you modify the tasks?

Do your common language tasks have:

1. Standard or uniform directions for administration?

2. Clear and comprehensible directions for students?

3. Relevant instructional assessment supports, such as illustrations or graphics?

4. Pleasing format and presentation of materials?

5. Language that challenges students at their given levels of language proficiency?

6. Opportunities for students to interact with each other?

7. Relevant and interesting activities for students?

8. Activities that require students to engage in higher-order thinking?

9. Opportunities for student self-assessment and reflection?

If necessary, how might you modify the tasks?

Based on your analysis, how might you devise an action plan to keep construction on schedule?

Activity 4.5
Pilot and Feedback From a Common Language Assessment Task

Teacher: _____

Grade: _____

Name of common language task: _____

Number of language learners at each language proficiency level: _____

_____

1. Did the common language assessment meet its intended purpose?

2. Which aspects or features of the common language assessment worked?

3. Does the common language assessment measure language learning? What evidence do you have?

4. How does the common language assessment inform instruction of language learners?

5. Which aspects of the common language assessment need clarification or revision?

Activity 4.6
Selecting Types of Rubrics and Documentation

First, note the common language tasks currently being constructed for a grade, language education program, or school. Next, scan the list of rubrics and documentation forms, and mark those you use in your classroom for instructional assessment. Repeat this activity, matching the common language tasks to their rubrics or documentation forms. Share your thinking with others to see if you agree as a group.

Language Task	Type of Rubric or Documentation	Used for Instructional Assessment	Used for Common Language Assessment
	Checklists		
	Rating scales		
	Holistic scales		
	Analytic scales		
	Project descriptors		
	Anecdotal notes		
	Narrative reports		
	Answer keys from tests		
	Matrices		
	Tallies		

Activity 4.7
Involving Students in Instructional Assessment

How might you expand the participation of language learners in language assessment? Here are some ideas that relate to the aspects of language assessment to share with your students. Don't forget—allow students with low levels of language proficiency to use their native language to gain an understanding of their expectations for the language task or project.

The big idea for this language task or project is:

The overall language target is:

Some ideas for language tasks are:

Some supports and resources that will help language learners are:

The language objectives for each group of language learners are:

- Beginner

- Intermediate

- Advanced

The ways to interpret or score student work are:

Chapter 5

Phase IV: Inspection

Truth is confirmed by inspection and delay; falsehood by haste and uncertainty.

—PUBLIUS CORNELIUS TACITUS

Having had opportunities to review the instructional assessment plan and modify the language tasks based on initial feedback, it is now time to think about how to analyze, interpret, and report the data. In addition, the information from the common language assessments will help refine the process and products that ultimately help improve teaching and learning.

Before becoming engrossed in the particulars of Phase IV, let's see how Mrs. Soto and her team approached the task of inspection.

Organizing Principle: Data from common language assessment must be relevant and meaningful for students, educators, and other stakeholders.

Lead Question: How can the educational community use information from common language assessment in beneficial ways?

Graham School: Inspecting the Results

The professional learning team was anxious to analyze the results of its common language assessments and benchmark the students' language proficiency. Each pair followed the steps for data analysis, from charting the language data to cataloguing the evidence. Mrs. Soto and her partner meticulously examined every student's oral language sample against the rubric's criteria. They had never thought of weighting the results, but when the advisor to the project helped the team understand the relationship between students' language development and its achievement, it made total sense.

Mrs. Soto, who had been working with family members throughout the project, took the lead in devising ways to report the results to family members. Being bilingual in Spanish and English, she chaired a schoolwide committee to locate bilingual individuals willing to volunteer to translate materials into Graham's major languages. Providing descriptive feedback to students was also part of the initial plan of the learning team; in this instance,

Mrs. Soto used Spanish with her Hispanic English learners and convinced volunteers, fluent in her English learners' other languages, to assist in her classroom.

The measurement unit informed Mrs. Soto's instruction by helping her become a more culturally responsive teacher. She realized, first of all, that instruction must connect to the students' lives. It was an easy adjustment to extend measurement to the metric system, and in doing so, it provided access to grade-level concepts for some of her English learners. Once the second-grade partners modified the task, it became apparent that Juan and Shama understood the concepts, but merely lacked the labels for them in English.

In addition, although skeptical at first, Mrs. Soto discovered the benefits of students interacting with each other during instruction, as long as assessment insisted on individual accountability. She remembered how Caryn, her student with a learning disability, listened attentively and understood when her classmate explained what to do, then always responded with a smile. Lastly, Mrs. Soto was amazed watching her students engage in self-assessment and came to understand that even seven-year-olds could take responsibility for their own learning.

Mrs. Soto gave her students individual oral feedback during the daily math lesson. She often repeated the language objective before giving each student a thumbs up or thumbs down, or asking her students to give an oral example that showed their understanding of the language of mathematics. Interpreting the final oral project was more complex, required more time and, most importantly, was undertaken by the professional learning team rather than individual teachers. The information from the results of the week-long project contributed to decision making for all second graders. For this reason, the school leaders busily prepared a presentation for the upcoming meeting with the local school council.

In the end, the second-grade pair created a task-specific holistic speaking rubric (table 5.1) to capture the language target. After getting feedback from the learning team, Mrs. Soto and her partner applied it in benchmarking the students' oral samples. The teachers were proud of the milestones that their students had reached.

The professional learning team was aware of the importance of descriptive feedback for the students. For each project or language task, partners gathered data to create exemplars. The following was Mrs. Soto's feedback to her low intermediate students: "You compared the different sizes of objects on your table, just like we did it together. Next time, I would like you to ask me, 'Which is longer, the pencil or the crayon?' and I will answer, 'The pencil is *longer than* the crayon.' Then it will be my turn to ask you a question."

Table 5.1: Task-Specific Holistic Rubric

Language Proficiency Level	The Measurement Project Oral Language Scale
5	Use grade-level oral discourse related to measurement. Provide reasons related to use of measurement tools and units. Use grade-level technical vocabulary related to measurement.
4	Use oral discourse related to measurement tools and units. Discuss comparative use of measurement tools and units. Use content-specific vocabulary for measurement tools and units.
3	Use relative clauses in complex oral sentences related to measurement tools and units. Evaluate effectiveness of use of measurement tools and units. Use content-related vocabulary for using measurement tools and units.
2	Use comparative language in simple oral sentences involving measurement tools and units. Ask and answer questions related to comparing measurement tools and units. Use general vocabulary related to using measurement tools and units.
1	Use words and phrases to identify measurement tools and units. Answer questions related to comparing measurement tools and units. Use general vocabulary-related measurement.

Based on the data on student feedback from the language tasks, the professional learning team established quarterly language goals. In goal statements, the learning target expanded to other contexts or content areas. The second-grade teachers went further by setting up student-teacher conferences to discuss the language goal and then translated it to send home. Here was one student language goal that Mrs. Soto and Juan agreed upon: "I am going to practice using sentences that compare two objects, two people, two places, or two events. *Voy a practicar usar oraciones que comparan dos objetos, dos personas, dos lugares, o dos eventos.*"

Take a couple of minutes to think of questions that may pertain to each topical area in Activity 5.1, Questions for Phase IV: Inspection (page 121, and online at **go.solution-tree.com/ELL**). Then check against the questions within the body of the chapter and add to the checklist in Activity 5.2, Checklist for Phase IV: Inspection (page 122 and online). Finally, proceed to Activity 5.3, People and Timeline for Phase IV: Inspection (page 123 and online), where you and your team have the opportunity to identify the persons, responsibilities, and timeframe for each step of this phase.

Questions for Phase IV: Inspection

During this phase, we take our first glimpse at the assessment data and decide how to communicate the results from common language assessment to different stakeholders. Most importantly, as professional learning teams, we spend time contemplating how the information from assessment might inform and improve our instruction of English learners.

Questions for Professional Learning Teams

A. Analysis and Interpretation of Data

1. What kinds of information do the rubrics, scoring forms, or project descriptors yield?

2. What are the scoring options for common language assessment, and which one is preferred?

3. What procedure can be used for benchmarking and monitoring students' language progress toward meeting language development standards?

4. What are the plans for data analysis and reporting?

5. What weights might be assigned to the results from language assessment?

B. Communication of the Results

1. How are results communicated in meaningful ways and in multiple languages?

2. How are the results contextualized in light of the unique characteristics of English learners?

3. How are results translated into descriptive feedback for students?

C. Use of Information

1. How does the information from common language assessment help subsequent student language learning?

2. How is information from common language assessment used to make instructional decisions?

3. How might students, or students in collaboration with their teachers, create individual language goals based on the results?

4. Based on the results, what modifications or improvements need to be made to the common language assessment?

The inspection phase invites professional learning teams, in collaboration with school or district personnel, to mine the data to determine the viability of the common language assessment. Meaningful and valid results from the language tasks or projects that provide information on the students' progress in language development move educators toward officially accepting and adopting the common language assessment.

Analysis and Interpretation of Data

Professional learning teams provide the foundational structure to plan, design, implement, and revise common language assessment; for this phase of construction these tightly knit educator groups become data teams (Ainsworth & Viegut, 2006). As we approach the last two phases of construction, inspection, and maintenance, data teams are vital to the continued functioning of common language assessment.

One of the first decisions in this phase is the selection of a scoring option for determining the performance of language learners.

Information From Rubrics

The choice of a rubric substantially influences the kinds of information that will be available for interpreting and reporting student performance. The extent to which the selected rubric is a good match for the language assessment determines the usefulness of the data it yields.

Let's revisit the rubrics presented in the refinement phase, but now let's think about the ways we can analyze and interpret the data. Table 5.2 (page 102) displays the types of rubrics and possible means of analysis. Some analyses, such as determining percent, for example, may apply to all types of rubrics; other analyses are unique to a particular rubric.

Take this opportunity to evaluate the effectiveness of the rubrics you are currently considering for your common language assessment. Review the list of rubrics and documentation forms for language assessment and the possible analyses displayed in table 5.1 (page 99). Then use Activity 5.4, Analyzing Information From Rubrics (page 124 and online), to match your preferred analyses to your selected rubrics for common language assessment.

Table 5.2: Types of Rubrics and Ways of Analyzing Information

Type of Rubric	Means of Analysis
Checklists	1. Tally number of correct/incorrect items to ascertain a raw score. 2. Determine percent of correct/incorrect items. 3. Determine percent of behaviors/skills that are present/absent.
Rating Scales	1. Calculate frequency of occurrence of each option. 2. Calculate quality of skills, strategies, or behaviors. 3. Calculate the mean or average score for individual students.
Holistic Scales	1. Rank student samples numerically. 2. Calculate mean or average score for groups of students. 3. Highlight evidence of criteria from level to level.
Analytic Scales	1. Create a profile of criteria by dimension. 2. Weigh the criteria by dimension, and add dimension scores to create a composite score. 3. Assign a score within a range according to the dimension, and total the assigned dimension scores.

Scoring Options

Depending on your school or district administration policy, professional learning teams can score common language tasks and assign performance levels to student work. When scoring occurs externally, outside the classroom or school, teachers are generally not directly involved in producing or reporting the results. Selected-response tests, such as multiple choice, can readily be scored manually or electronically with a scoring key, while constructed-response questions, such as writing samples, can be shipped out to an independent contractor or be regionally scored.

On the other hand, when scoring is internal to a district or school, special arrangements must be made to ensure a timely and organized analysis of student samples. In this scenario, teachers should not score their own students' language tasks but instead recruit teacher representatives from participating schools. Other options include: (1) professional learning teams could form scoring teams, (2) schools could elicit the assistance of data coaches, (3) grade-level teachers could partner, or (4) retired teachers could volunteer to help. Table 5.3 outlines the advantages and disadvantages of each scoring option.

Professional development around the scoring of performance assessment of language learners offers educators insight into how students process and produce language in relation to how they achieve academically. By gaining an understanding of what students can do at various levels of language proficiency, teachers can better focus on individual student needs. In addition, benchmarking is a well worthwhile process for professional learning or data teams to undertake as part of building common language assessment.

Table 5.3: Pros and Cons of Scoring Options for Common Language Assessment

	Advantages	Disadvantages
Externally scored common language assessment	No investment in teacher time Strong reliability of results Often a quick return of results	Almost exclusive use of selected-response items Expensive, if electronically scored or subcontracted May only be feasible in large school districts
Internally scored common language assessment	Increased opportunities for teacher collaboration Rich professional development for educators who gain insight into student performance Direct connection of results to instruction	May be difficult to coordinate Professional development on assessment literacy necessary Teachers need for practice to establish inter-rater agreement on student work Time a possible issue

Benchmarking Common Language Assessment

Recently, we have heard the term *benchmarking* in reference to the state-led initiative of developing Common Core State Standards that are competitive internationally and benchmarked against students in high-performing nations around the world (Darling-Hammond, 2010). In this instance, a benchmark can be equated with a point of reference. Benchmarking in regard to common language assessment carries slightly different interpretations and uses.

In one case, benchmarks are products, generally selected measures purchased from commercial vendors, that are administered at predetermined times during the school year. The primary purpose of a benchmark test is to predict the extent students are on the pathway toward meeting accountability targets determined by annual state tests. The data from benchmark measures are often correlated with state accountability measures to determine the relationship between the two sets of scores and the trajectory for students in meeting state standards. The higher the correlate, the greater the chance students (schools and districts) will meet accountability requirements. Benchmarking for the purpose of predicting student performance can occur in conjunction with common, interim, or standardized forms of assessment.

On the other hand, benchmarking may be viewed as a process in which student performance is examined against standards-referenced expectations. The purpose of this benchmarking is to monitor students' progress using local data, grade by grade within a school, across multiple schools within a district. In this instance, benchmarking may be determined by the administration of a school district which has set predetermined instructional targets. It may also be viewed from a professional development perspective that involves professional learning teams, teachers, and school leaders setting the performance bar.

In this interpretation, benchmarks are often points on a scale or criteria of a rubric that correspond to attainable goals for students. These points represent incremental progressions defined by clear descriptors that differentiate levels of performance on instructional assessment tasks or projects. This means of benchmarking is tied to progress monitoring of students during a school year and provides teachers immediate results for redirecting instruction.

Turning now to common language assessment, for benchmarking to be consistent and effective, the same metric has to be applied to the language tasks each time. For example, student writing samples must be scored against the same criteria in a rubric in the same manner. Because we are approaching benchmarking from a practitioner's rather than a test developer's perspective, certain steps should be taken to maximize information gained about student performance.

Benchmarking Common Language Assessment Using Rubrics

Preparation prior to benchmarking involves using specified criteria in rubrics. Since language tasks are designed for English learners, so, too, the criteria in the rubrics are language features. To begin the benchmarking process, first inspect the rubric or scoring guide to ensure that it is:

- Teacher- (and student-) friendly
- Clear in its criteria or descriptors
- Versatile, so that it can be applied to multiple language tasks
- Reflective of language development
- Comprehensive in its coverage of levels
- Representative of the range of performance of English learners
- Capable of capturing what English learners can do

Second, finalize the selection of the rubric, scoring guide, or documentation form to use with common language assessment. To reach consensus on the selection of the rubric or scoring guide:

- Pilot various language rubrics or scoring guides, and make adjustments based on work samples of English learners and proficient English students
- Verify that the rubric represents the language tasks, language targets, and language development standards to be measured
- Be sure all feel comfortable and confident using the rubric

In anticipation of scoring students' samples from common language assessment, teachers and administrators should become well versed in the criteria of the selected rubric. Professional learning teams need to have undergone a substantial amount of preparation to organize the scoring event if it is going to be conducted within the school or district. The following activities are important precursors to benchmarking performance assessment:

- Reach consensus on identifying student "anchor" papers—those papers that represent the midpoint of each scoring point or performance level; a five-point scale, for example, has five anchors.

- Select range-finder papers that illustrate the plus and minus side of each anchor paper; on a five-point scale there are range-finder papers that represent 1+, 2-, 2+, 3-, 3+, 4-, 4+, and 5-.

- Come to acceptable levels of inter-rater agreement on the performance level of student samples (generally, acceptable means 80 percent to 90 percent of raters agree on the exact and adjacent levels).

Chapter 6 describes in detail the procedures on how to reach acceptable levels of inter-rater agreement. High levels of inter-rater agreement are a sign of reliability from rater to rater on student samples from performance assessment. Consequently, educators can have confidence in the assigned scores and can move forward in the benchmarking process.

Benchmarking Language Proficiency

Language proficiency benchmarks delineate students' language progress along a developmental scale for listening, speaking, reading, or writing. Benchmarking common language assessment should always be based on student scores in relation to language development standards. Activity 5.5, Considerations Prior to Benchmarking (page 125 and online), presents a checklist for benchmarking language proficiency data.

Keeping the language target and common language tasks or projects in mind, a starting point for benchmarking student performance is the selection of a rubric or documentation form. Working together, benchmark common language assessment using the following steps:

1. Decide to use a standards matrix of language development or a rubric that teachers have found effective for interpreting English learners' language proficiency.

2. Set the benchmarks, or language proficiency levels, attainable for each subgroup of English learners for the language task.

3. Score student work against the language target using the rubric, and establish inter-rater agreement.

4. Determine whether students have attained the benchmark or have made progress toward reaching the benchmark, based on their level of English language proficiency.

Graham School: Revisiting the Measurement Project

The second-grade team was preparing to benchmark the results from the common language assessment on measurement. They reviewed the language target and the instructional sequence that consisted of a series of three scaffolded tasks. Then they examined a holistic and analytic rubric to use with the project. Here are the steps Mrs. Soto and her partner took in implementing the three tasks, selecting a rubric, and analyzing the results.

Language Target (from Language Development Standards): *Use the language of measurement and its associated tools in real-life situations, such as in comparing the dimensions of a room.*

Thematic Big Idea: *Measurement tools help us design the world around us.*

Task 1: Experiment With Measurement

Students, in partners, chose nonstandard and standard (for example, number lines, rulers, yardsticks, meter sticks) tools to measure a selection of classroom objects, such as tables, desks, and bookcases. They alternated between asking and answering questions using comparative language, modeled by the teacher, for each measurement. Mrs. Soto then built on the students' language by first showing, and then asking, the more proficient speakers to use relative phrases to estimate or predict lengths or widths of objects. Midway through the week, students experimented with standard measurement tools in estimating the perimeter of polygons.

Task 2: Maintain Learning and Language Logs of Drawings and Notes

Students drew the dimensions and recorded the lengths and widths in their learning logs, according to their standard measurement tools. They submitted entries in an interactive language journal on what they discovered when experimenting with different tools as well as their personal reactions and reflections. Throughout the course of the week, Mrs. Soto gave descriptive oral or written feedback to each student on his or her individual language objectives.

Task 3: Create a Display of a Room and Give an Oral Talk

In this second-grade project, common language assessment students had an opportunity to be architects or carpenters in designing and measuring a room of their choice. In partners (an English learner and a proficient English speaker or a Spanish learner and a proficient Spanish speaker), students selected various standard measurement tools (for example, number lines, rulers, yardsticks, or meter sticks). They were invited to be as inventive or creative as they wished in designing and furnishing a room using their measurement tools.

The common language task, the oral talk, was geared to the students' level of language proficiency. Students discussed how they used standard tools in designing and measuring their space and provided details on why they selected standard tools for measuring different objects.

Evidence of Performance

Each student's oral talk was videotaped and interpreted by Mrs. Soto and her partner content teacher using the project rubric. These documentation forms captured the three benchmarks for language proficiency, differentiated by language proficiency levels that reflected the language target. The teachers agreed on each student's language proficiency level and more than 90 percent of the time provided specific evidence to support their decision.

Table 5.4 is the holistic project rubric used for interpreting oral evidence from designing and measuring a room. Based on the language the student produced, Mrs. Soto highlighted those criteria that were clearly evident and then circled the student's language proficiency level, from 1 to 5, or assigned a mid level (such as 2.5), if evidence crossed two contiguous levels. It was followed by a matrix on the language of measurement; for the oral report, only the dimension on speaking was used. Table 5.5 (page 109) is the analytic rubric that shows the four language domains for the project.

Table 5.4: A Holistic Rubric for the Measurement Project

Language Proficiency Level	Performance on the Oral Language Measurement Project
5	Use grade-level oral discourse related to measurement. Use grade-level technical vocabulary for using measurement and data.
4	Use oral discourse related to comparing room dimensions. Use content-specific vocabulary for using measurement and data.
3	Use relative clauses in complex oral sentences to predict measurement. Use content-related vocabulary for using measurement and data.
2	Use comparative language in simple oral sentences involving standard measurement. Use general vocabulary related to solving measurement problems.
1	Use words and phrases to identify standard measurement tools. Use general vocabulary related to measurement.

Table 5.5: Using a Standards-Based Language Proficiency Matrix to Set Benchmarks for Common Language Assessment

English Language Proficiency Standard: English learners communicate information, ideas, and concepts necessary for academic success in the content area of mathematics.

Grade-Level Cluster: 1–2
Example Content Topic: Standard measurement tools

Language Domain	Language Proficiency Level 1	Language Proficiency Level 2	Language Proficiency Level 3	Language Proficiency Level 4	Language Proficiency Level 5
Listening	Evaluate and select real-life standard measurement tools.	Evaluate the effectiveness of real-life standard measurement tools in various situations.	Evaluate the use of different real-life standard measurement tools.	Evaluate the application of real-life standard measurement tools to various situations.	Evaluate designs made from standard measurement tools.
Speaking	Name real-life standard measurement tools and objects.	Compare size (for example, length and width) using real-life standard measurement tools.	Predict how real-life standard measurement tools might be used in various situations.	Discuss uses of real-life standard measurement tools in various situations.	Give details on why standard tools are used for measuring different objects.
Reading	Use diagrams or icons to guide standard measurement of familiar objects with a partner.	Use labeled diagrams or icons from texts to guide standard measurement of objects with a partner.	Use key phrases in illustrated text in standard measurement of objects with a partner.	Use sentences in illustrated text in standard measurement of objects with a partner.	Use a series of sentences in illustrated text in standard measurement of objects with a partner.
Writing	Create and label illustrated examples or displays of standard measurement with a partner.	Create and describe illustrated examples or displays of standard measurement with a partner.	Create and evaluate illustrated examples or displays of standard measurement with a partner.	Create and explain illustrated examples of how to problem solve using standard measurement with a partner.	Create and narrate illustrated stories around problem solving using standard measurement with a partner.

Source: Adapted from the Board of Regents of the University of Wisconsin System (2007) on behalf of the World-Class Instructional Design and Assessment Consortium, Wisconsin Center for Education Research, University of Wisconsin, Madison. Used with permission.

Even though schools and districts are data rich, many have not had conversations on information from common language assessment. Language proficiency data, along with achievement data, help the educational community gain personal insight into how to improve the instruction and performance of language learners.

As part of constructing common language assessment, professional learning teams can engage in the process of benchmarking. Activity 5.6, Benchmarking Common Language Assessment From Start to Finish (page 126 and online), exemplifies the step-by-step process of benchmarking language proficiency for English learners. Prior to now, educator teams may have completed steps 1 to 3; they can use this opportunity as a way of inspecting their common language assessments.

Data Analysis: A Multistep Process

Constructing common language assessment, collecting data on the assessment, and setting benchmarks for language proficiency of language learners are precursors to conducting data analyses. Larry Ainsworth and Donald Viegut (2006) suggest a systematic data-driven decision-making model for data teams. This five-step process is intended to assist teachers to better differentiate instruction for their students and provide timely feedback to their students. We adapt it here based on data from common language assessment and add a sixth step to ensure communicating the results to students and other stakeholders.

Step 1: Chart the Data From Common Language Assessment

Visibly plotting the language data onto a graph, chart, or table makes it come to life. Options for retrieving the data from common language assessment include securing it from: (1) a computer program, (2) a school or district server, (3) a school-based Excel spreadsheet, or (4) a written record or form. In this first step, organize the data with the intent of determining the number or percent of students or subgroups of students who have met the preset benchmark.

When inspecting language proficiency data, benchmarks are generally set at language proficiency levels and can be readily displayed with a bar graph or histogram. Figure 5.1 (page 110) illustrates how results from common language assessment might appear graphically. This is a simulated histogram with data for English language proficiency (ELP) based on five proficiency levels for a hypothetical cohort of 100 English learners in grades 3, 4, and 5.

Step 2: Interpret the Results in Reference to Standards and Student Characteristics

In reviewing language proficiency data, the first questions to ask are how many benchmarks need to be set, and do they indicate that language learners have met language development targets? Perhaps one benchmark represents the point where English learners no longer need language support. If language proficiency (ELP) level 4 has been selected as the cutoff point for attaining full language proficiency, then the following statements can be made about the students' performance based on the data display in figure 5.1.

- Thirty-five percent of third and fifth graders reached or exceeded the benchmark, while 30 percent of fourth graders did so.

- Thirty percent of third graders, 35 percent of fourth graders, and 38 percent of fifth graders are approaching attainment of the benchmark.

- Thirty-five percent of third graders, 35 percent of fifth graders, and 27 percent of fifth graders are at the beginning stages of English language development.

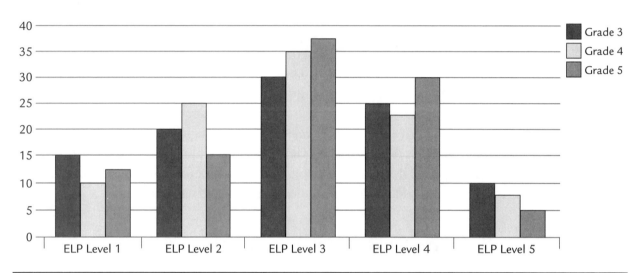

Figure 5.1: A hypothetical bar graph of the distribution of the number of English learners at each level of English language proficiency for grades 3, 4, and 5.

Language proficiency data reveal how much, not how well, English learners have developed English. No judgment or evaluation about the students, their teachers, or their language education program should be made from these data without knowing student characteristics and circumstances. Returning to the bar graph as an example of a display of language proficiency data:

- We have only one source of information (and decisions should always be based on evidence from multiple measures).

- We do not know the background of the students (and students' prior experiences are going to impact their performance).

- We do not know the initial language proficiency levels of the students (and determining growth minimally requires two data points).

- We have no information on the language education program.

- We have no information on the qualifications of the teachers serving these students.

If, in fact, there are large numbers of language learners distributed across the entire continuum of second language development, multiple benchmarks may be set. For example, there may be a subgroup of newcomers at the beginning levels of English language development and another subgroup of long-term English learners at the mid-levels. In this case, there might be two benchmarks set that correspond to the differentiated language objectives of the instructional assessment project and each group of students' levels of English language development.

Step 3: Share the Findings With Stakeholders

Since common language assessment is meant to describe language learning to better foster teaching and learning, engage other stakeholders in the conversation. The place to start this dialog is with the teachers and students affected by assessment results; they are best positioned to determine subsequent data targets, as shown in Step 4 (page 112). Other stakeholder groups should also stay abreast of how findings from language assessment can help inform language instruction.

Sharing of findings from the data analysis must fit the audience, whether individual students, parents, teachers, school leaders, or boards of education. There must be consideration of where and how data are to be presented. For example, graphs and charts embedded in a PowerPoint show may be ideal for boards of education, while explanations in family members' native language, along with data displays, may best suit students and parents. Table 5.6 suggests venues for presentation of results from data analyses of common language assessment for different stakeholders.

Table 5.6: How Results From Common Language Assessment May Be Communicated to Stakeholders

Stakeholder Group	Venues for Presentation of Results
Students	In student-teacher conferences With family members at a school's open house
Parents/Family Members	In student-teacher-family conferences On teacher websites, blogs, or information logs
Teachers	At grade-level meetings During collaboration time between language and content teachers As part of a professional development series
School Leaders	At cabinet-level meetings in the school district At school faculty meetings
Boards of Education	At monthly school board meetings In school district newsletters or websites

Based on the analyses and interpretation of results, each stakeholder group may give input into setting subsequent data targets, starting with professional learning teams.

Step 4: Set Data Targets

Now that the data have been displayed and analyzed, we need to determine whether enough students have hit the preset benchmark. In order to do so, formulate a statement to estimate the projected performance of language learners in relation to the benchmark. Statements such as in figure 5.2 use the results from common language assessment to create realistic data targets for language development, differentiated by the students' language proficiency levels.

Sample Data Targets for Language Development

_____ (number) or _____ percent of_____ English learners at English language proficiency level _____ will maintain or increase their performance by _____ percent of a language proficiency level in the language domain(s) of_____ starting from _____ (date of last common language assessment) to the end of _____ (date of current language assessment).

A Common Language Assessment Target for Dual Language Development

_____ (number) or _____ percent of_____ language learners at language proficiency level _____ in English will maintain or increase their performance by _____ percent of a language proficiency level; and those in language proficiency level _____ in their other language will increase their performance by _____ percent of a language proficiency level in their other language starting from _____ (date of last common language assessment) to the end of _____ (date of current language assessment).

Source: Adapted from Common Formative Assessments: How to Connect Standards-Based Instruction and Assessment *(2006), by Larry Ainsworth and Donald Viegut. Thousand Oaks, CA: Corwin Press. Reprinted with permission.*

Figure 5.2: Communicating language targets for English language development and dual language development.

Step 5: Select and Implement Instructional Strategies or Interventions

The results from common language assessment guide the selection of instructional strategies to address the linguistic challenges students face. Certain strategies or interventions may apply to RTI policies and procedures specific to English learners. It is of utmost importance to consider proven strategies that have evidence of effectiveness for this student population for the students' given levels of English language proficiency. Provide coaching, mentoring, or additional opportunities for professional development on the English learner strategies for teachers who are not well-versed in best practices for students who are participating in common language assessment.

Step 6: Identify Evidence of Effectiveness

The evidence of effectiveness of the instructional strategies rests on the data from the second, third, even fourth rounds of common language assessment, provided the identical rubric or scoring guide is used and teachers reach acceptable levels of inter-rater agreement on student samples. Evidence of student performance should reflect the extent to which the language target is met, which, in turn, relates back to language development standards.

We have come full circle in the process of data analysis, beginning and ending with common language assessment. Figure 5.3 is a summary of the steps that lead to and involve the examination of data from common language assessment.

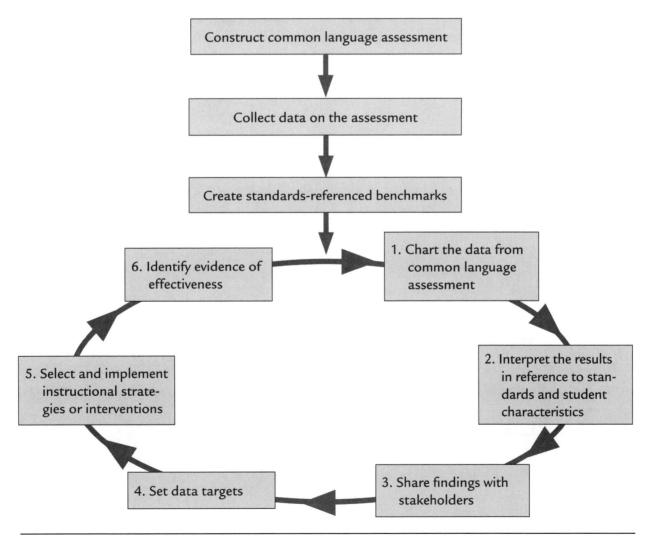

Figure 5.3: Steps in the analysis of student data from common language assessment.

How would you conduct data analysis for your common language tasks or projects? Activity 5.7, Analyzing Data From Common Language Assessment (page 127 and online), sets up the six steps of data analysis to complete.

Weighting results from assessment allows educators to better understand the context of student performance. In the case of English learners, for example, when the assessment is in English, English language proficiency should be weighted against the results of academic achievement. In that way, students are not penalized for not having the requisite language in English to access content.

Weighting Results From Common Language Assessment for Language Learners

Weighting assessment results enables educators to assign relative value for each dimension of a language domain, such as speaking or writing, to more realistically portray student performance. More importantly, the notion of weighting ensures a greater connection between assessment and instruction for language learners. For example, the Student Oral Language Observation Matrix (SOLOM) is a focused analytic language proficiency rubric that has been used for decades to measure English learners' oral production. In it, oral language development is defined by five dimensions—comprehension, fluency, vocabulary, pronunciation, and grammar—across five levels of language proficiency. In scoring students' oral language samples, each dimension of the rubric assumes an equal weight, assuming a 20 percent value. Ideally, each dimension should be adjusted to reflect the emphases of the language curriculum of the school or district. When added together, the five dimensions should still total 100 percent, but the percentages should be distributed to represent curricular goals.

Activity 5.8, Weighting an Analytic Scale to Match Language Curricular Goals (page 128 and online), is intended to prompt deep discussion and provide an opportunity for teams to reach consensus on the relative importance of different dimensions of multidimensional rubrics. Consider assigning weights to analytic scales so that they better correspond to what is valued in teaching. Having decided on how to assign weights to scores, the next step is to communicate the results to the greater educational community.

Communication of the Results

Teachers and school leaders must make information from assessment understandable to other stakeholders. When thinking about how best to communicate results from common language assessment, realize that family members of English learners who come from diverse linguistic and cultural backgrounds may not:

- Have been schooled in the United States or Canada and therefore may not be familiar with how the school system operates
- Be knowledgeable of the culture of schooling

- Be well-versed or literate in English and have varying degrees of literacy in their native language
- Be available to come to school as they hold multiple jobs
- Understand standards-referenced education
- Have access to a computer or be technologically savvy

Every attempt should be made to embrace family members and bring linguistic and cultural diversity into the school community. By feeling welcome and gaining an understanding of the expectations of their children's language development, family members can become contributors to the success of a school. Here are some ideas for communicating the results from common language assessment in meaningful ways to family members:

- Create reports that are not literacy dependent and are easy to understand.
- Design a report template that is readily translatable into the languages of family members.
- Consider printing side-by-side reports with the identical information in two languages, English and the primary language of the family members.
- Use icons alongside key words or expressions, such as for the four language domains, to facilitate understanding.
- Use graphs, histograms, or other visuals to indicate a student's performance in relation to language development standards.
- Conduct home visits and spend some time discussing the results with family members.
- Set times during the day or week when bilingual staff are available and open to talking to or working with family members.
- Make your classroom open and inviting to family members.

Contextualizing the Results for English Learners

Results from common language assessment have little meaning in themselves. Often, decisions are based on unsubstantiated evidence or results from a single measure. Unless the results operate within a greater educational context, their interpretation may be narrow and misleading. Change within a school or district, such as turnover of school leaders and personnel, the mobility of students, or the arrival of new waves of refugees, may help explain student performance in a report. To make results from common language assessment meaningful, stakeholders should consider the performance of English learners in relation to the:

- Students' levels of language proficiency
- Data from other language proficiency measures
- Amount of language support given during instruction and assessment
- Students' previous performance on language tasks

- Standards-referenced language targets
- Language education program in which students participate

Offering language learners feedback on what they can do and what they may need to work on is helpful in advancing the students' understanding of their expectations for learning.

Providing Descriptive Feedback for Students

Data from common language assessment help inform instructional practice and help teachers monitor students' language progress. In its formative capacity, these data should be used to give descriptive feedback to students in relation to the language target (Ainsworth & Viegut, 2006; Moss & Brookhart, 2009; Popham; 2008).

With its ultimate goal of furthering student learning, teachers may provide feedback to students through multiple modalities; it may be oral, written, or performance, depending on its appropriateness for the task or students. For English learners, a combination of modalities may be most beneficial. Teachers could model feedback with gestures while simultaneously reinforcing it orally, in the students' native language or English. Teachers could also provide written feedback that could be paraphrased orally for students.

The following are suggestions of how to provide effective feedback to English learners:

1. Consider the student's developmental, language proficiency, and experiential levels (be realistic).
2. Compare the student's performance to the language target and related standard (be objective).
3. Begin with a description of what the student did well (be positive).
4. Suggest a follow-up strategy for the student to try (be supportive).
5. Make sure the student understands what is expected (be clear).

Graham School: Oral Feedback

During the instructional assessment unit, Mrs. Soto provided descriptive feedback to her students as they worked on task 1 and task 2 (remember task 3 was used as common language assessment). Students at English language proficiency level 2 were expected to use certain targeted phrases to compare size using real-life measurement tools. Mrs. Soto provided oral feedback to Juan by saying, "You compared the different sizes of objects in your desk, just as we did together. Next time, I would like you to tell me, 'The pencil is longer than the crayon.' You also could say, 'The crayon is shorter than the pencil!'"

Feedback is a powerful instructional assessment tool that enhances learning (Marzano, 2006). Offering positive, descriptive feedback to students is a motivator for them to continue on the path of growth and achievement.

Use of Information

If stakeholders do not find the data useful, then the assessment has not made a difference. Here are some ideas on how to promote sound educational practices from language data. Teachers can:

- Plan or adjust language lessons and units based on results
- Set language targets
- Collaborate with peers on how to differentiate instruction and assessment
- Coach fellow teachers on specified language criteria or engage in reciprocal teaching
- Share evidenced-based language teaching strategies
- Dedicate time to meet with grade-level teams
- Include school leadership in data-led discussions
- Promote schoolwide awareness of the performance of language learners

To further their language learning, students need to have ownership of their data, understand the meaning of assessment results, and convert those findings into action steps. Here are some ideas for how students may use assessment data. English learners can:

- Contribute to their individual goal setting
- Check their results against language criteria
- Track their personal language development
- Explain their language performance over time at student-teacher conferences

Another important use of data from common language assessment is to aid teachers, students, and other stakeholders in decision making.

Making Data-Driven Decisions

Educational decisions should always be based on accrued evidence from multiple measures and multiple sources collected over multiple points in time. Whereas data from high-stakes annual assessments impact district and state accountability, at the other end of the spectrum, classroom-based evidence allows individual teachers to make decisions about their own students. Between these two ends, data from common language assessment may offset that of the district or be helpful in making periodic local decisions at the school or program levels. Figure 5.4 (page 118) shows how the kinds of decisions made in an educational setting rely on data from different forms of assessment.

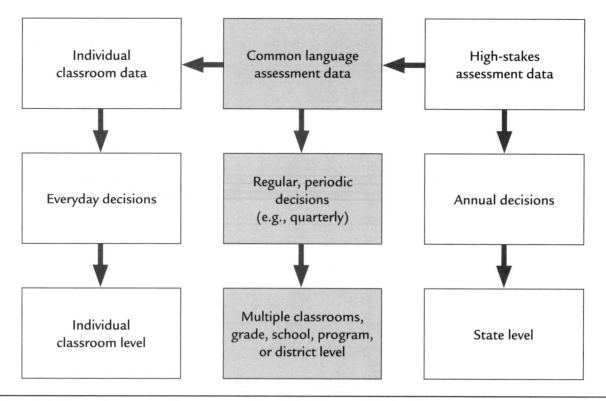

Figure 5.4: Connections among data sources, kinds of decisions, and levels of implementation.

What kinds of decisions are best made with data from common language assessment? Consider the following choices available to teachers and school leaders:

- Grouping language learners
- Mapping curriculum
- Planning units of instruction
- Differentiating language instruction and assessment
- Using languages other than English as media of instruction
- Measuring language targets
- Designing language education programs

Since, historically, much of the assessment data on English learners has not been particularly valid, educators should pay attention to information available through common language assessment. The accuracy and currency of these data facilitate creating student-level language goals.

Revisiting Language Targets

Assessment results from common language tasks enable educators to pinpoint students' strengths and challenges. Take time to analyze language data to get a clear picture of what English learners have accomplished and what they ought to focus on next. Together, perhaps on a quarterly basis that corresponds to a grading period, students and teachers should examine the data and revisit language targets. Feedback from the common language assessment may also help shape the discussion.

The data from common language assessment contribute to students' language targets and enable professional learning teams to reflect on the language tasks and re-examine the assessment plan.

Graham School: Sharing Language Targets

Mrs. Soto thought that parent-teacher conferences were the best time to share individual student data collected during instructional assessment. Not only did she explain her students' performance using a rubric, the parents also saw their children give oral reports by watching the video. The family members, students, and Mrs. Soto then discussed and formulated a language target. Based on the language data, the following language target was agreed upon: Juan will use comparative phrases to describe relationships between two objects, people, or events in sentences, extended sentences, or oral discourse.

Revisiting Common Language Tasks

Professional learning teams, in conjunction with school administrations, may conclude that common language tasks, having yielded such rich information and having been so enthusiastically embraced by students and teachers, should be recycled for the following school year. By repeating the common language assessment for two years with different groups of students from the same grade and language proficiency levels, cross-sectional data are produced; if the cycle becomes three years long, then trend data emerge. Having long-term data on students' language development is tremendously helpful in strategic planning of programs, schools, and districts.

On the other hand, data analysis and interpretation may point to a language task that was not as stimulating, meaningful, or effective for a designated group of language learners. Here is an opportunity to pool your resources to improve the assessment. Having both quantitative and qualitative evidence of how the language task is operating gives insight into the final set of changes that may be needed.

Recap of the Inspection Phase

The inspection phase of common language assessment affords professional learning teams time to review what has been built in light of the data that have been collected. In this phase, we closely scrutinize what has been done to date to ensure that construction has been following the right course.

Here are the critical steps undertaken during this phase:

1. Match language-centered rubrics to the language tasks.
2. Interpret students' work samples using the rubrics.
3. Create benchmarks as milestones for common language assessment.
4. Follow the multistep data analysis process.
5. Consider weighting results by language learners' levels of language proficiency.
6. Communicate standards-referenced results to stakeholders.

As you review the data, one last major hurdle lies ahead—making sure that the common language assessment is a reliable and valid measure of student performance.

Building Blocks

This chapter's Organizing Principle stresses the importance of meaningful data from common language assessment for language learners, their teachers, and other stakeholders. To ascertain the usefulness of the data, we first inspect rubrics and other documentation forms as a means of interpreting student performance. We examine the notion of benchmarking to help establish a standards-based reference of language progress and explore the usefulness for weighting results.

Having confidence in the results, we then move to how to communicate the information to students, family members, and the community at large. When appropriate, we translate results into graphs, charts, and other languages so that the data are readily understood and contextualized, keeping in mind the features of language learners. And we provide students both formative information, in the form of descriptive feedback, and summative information, in the form of standards or criteria-referenced grades.

Throughout the inspection phase of construction, we emphasize the overall usefulness of information from common language assessment. In particular, we see how information from language assessment can help to make standards-referenced curricular choices and instructional decisions, create language goals and targets, as well as further teaching and learning. The data also offer insight into the effectiveness of the language tasks, with ample opportunity to modify or improve them.

With inspection complete, we now are ready to preserve common language assessment with the final phase of construction, maintenance.

Activity 5.1
Questions for Phase IV: Inspection

Let's turn to inspecting the data, communicating the results, and using the information to improve what we do in schools. What additional questions do you have that relate to your specific context?

A. Analysis and Interpretation of Data

B. Communication of the Results

C. Use of Information

Activity 5.2
Checklist for Phase IV: Inspection

The questions pertaining to the inspection phase have been converted to commands that may serve as an ongoing checklist to help direct the development of common language assessment. If you wish, adapt the questions or comments you have generated for Activity 5.1, and add them to the checklist.

A. Analysis and Interpretation of Data

☐ Select scoring options for common language assessment, and make sure they yield useful information.

☐ Determine a procedure for benchmarking and determining student progress toward meeting language development standards.

☐ Analyze data and report findings.

☐ Weigh results from common language assessment to help explain the performance of language learners.

B. Communication of the Results

☐ Communicate results in meaningful ways and in multiple languages.

☐ Contextualize results in light of the unique characteristics of English learners.

☐ Translate results into descriptive feedback for students.

C. Use of Information

☐ Use information to help further students' language learning.

☐ Use information for making instructional decisions.

☐ Provide opportunities to students, or students in collaboration with their teachers, to create language goals based on the results.

☐ Modify language tasks or projects based on the results.

Activity 5.3
People and Timeline for Phase IV: Inspection

Brainstorm together the activities required and decisions to be made for the maintenance phase of construction.

Activities and Decisions	Beginning and Ending Dates	Person(s) Responsible
A. Analysis and Interpretation of Data		
A.1		
A.2		
A.3		
A.4		
B. Communication of the Results		
B.1		
B.2		
B.3		
B.4		
C. Use of Information		
C.1		
C.2		
C.3		
C.4		

Activity 5.4
Analyzing Information From Rubrics

Think about the kind of information rubrics yield in relation to the common language assessment tasks. Here are three easy steps to follow in your learning team. First, match your language task or project to a rubric. Then, discuss the kind of information you would find most beneficial for the given purpose of the assessment. Third, using table 5.1 (page 99) as a guide, select one or two ways in which the data from the rubric are to be analyzed.

Grade: _____

Date: _____

Team: _____

Type of Rubric	Language Task or Project	Information for Decision Making	Ways of Analyzing and Interpreting Information
Checklists			
Rating Scales			
Holistic Scales			
Analytic Scales			

Activity 5.5
Considerations Prior to Benchmarking

In preparation for benchmarking, ensure that the rubric or scoring guide represents the language task that is being measured and that there are sufficient quantities of student samples. Use this checklist in anticipation of a benchmarking event.

The rubric or scoring guide is:

☐ Teacher- (and student-) friendly

☐ Clear in its criteria or descriptors at each score point

☐ Versatile, so that it can be applied to multiple language tasks

☐ Used to interpret specific language domains or overall language proficiency

☐ Comprehensive, in having a wide enough range of levels for benchmarking

☐ Representative of what language learners can do

Teachers and administrators have:

☐ Reached consensus on the selection of the rubric or scoring guide

☐ Verified that the rubric represents the language tasks, learning targets, and standards to be measured

☐ Chosen student anchor papers and range finders for each scoring point

Activity 5.6
Benchmarking Common Language Assessment From Start to Finish

Use this activity as a template or guide for benchmarking common language assessment for language learners.

1. Select a standards-referenced language rubric for language learners.

2. Set the benchmark(s) based on the rubric.

3. Score student work against the rubric.

4. Determine the extent to which the students have reached the benchmark.

Activity 5.7
Analyzing Data From Common Language Assessment

Use this activity as a template or guide for setting up the analysis of data.

1. Chart the data from common language assessment.

2. Interpret the results in reference to standards and student characteristics.

3. Share the findings with stakeholders.

4. Set data targets.

5. Select and implement instructional strategies or interventions.

6. Identify evidence of effectiveness.

Activity 5.8
Weighting an Analytic Scale to Match Language Curricular Goals

What weights might you assign to each dimension of this listening comprehension rubric for English learners?

Dimension of Listening Comprehension	Language Proficiency Level			
	1. Beginner	**2. Intermediate**	**3. Advanced**	**4. Expert**
Understanding Spoken Language	Process short utterances of social language. Begin to comprehend with graphic or sensory support.	Process extended social and some academic language. Comprehend with graphic or sensory support.	Process multiple discourses of social and academic language. Comprehend without reliance on support.	Fully process social and academic language. Comprehend on par with proficient peers.
Responding to Oral Directions	Follow one-step oral commands. Respond to simple requests.	Follow multistep oral directions. Respond to requests made by familiar persons.	Follow multistep instructions embedded in discourse. Respond to requests made by unfamiliar persons.	Follow complex instructions similar to proficient peers. Respond to discourse from varied technologies.
Using Listening Strategies	Associate sounds and words with meaning. Use manipulatives or real-life materials to illustrate comprehension.	Focus on key words or chunks within the utterance. Use manipulatives, real-life materials, or writing to illustrate comprehension.	Attend to context to gain understanding of the message. Use visual and graphic support to aid, not show, comprehension.	Use a variety of strategies to maximize understanding of oral language. Use visual and graphic support to emphasize points.

page 1 of 2

Dimension of Listening Comprehension	Language Proficiency Level			
	1. Beginner	**2. Intermediate**	**3. Advanced**	**4. Expert**
Overall Listening Comprehension	Begin to show explicit comprehension when support is present. Respond to simple oral commands, statements, or social courtesies.	Demonstrate explicit comprehension when support is present. Respond to multistep oral directions and instructions.	Begin to demonstrate implicit comprehension when support is present. Respond to extended oral discourse.	Demonstrate implicit comprehension comparable to peers. Respond to discourse with literal and figurative language.

Source: Adapted from Assessing English Language Learners: Bridges from Language Proficiency to Academic Achievement *(2006), by Margo M. Gottlieb. Thousand Oaks, CA: Corwin Press. Reproduced with permission.*

Phase V: Maintenance

Another flaw in the human character is that everyone wants to build and no one wants to do maintenance.

—KURT VONNEGUT, JR.

Over the last chapters, we have seen our vision for building common language assessment for English learners become a reality. As we enter the final phase of construction, maintenance, we consider how and where the data are to be stored and retrieved, as well as the overall technical qualities of the assessment. To ensure the endurance of our efforts, we integrate common language assessment into the general education system where, informed by fair and useful data, all students have opportunities to thrive.

Organizing Principle: Common language assessment consists of reliable and valid tools embedded in an assessment system that supports continuous teaching and learning.

Lead Question: How are data from common language assessment for language learners integrated into, managed, and maintained within the greater educational system?

As is now routine, take a couple of minutes to generate a set of questions for each of the three topical areas; use the questions in Activity 6.1, Last Chance! (in reproducible form on page 147, and online at **go.solution-tree.com/ELL**) for this purpose. Then, as you work through the chapter, use the Checklist for Phase V: Maintenance in Activity 6.2 (page 148 and online) as a guide; finally, proceed to Activity 6.3, People and Timeline for Phase V: Maintenance (page 149 and online).

Let's look in on how Graham School handled the maintenance of common language assessment.

Graham School: Focusing on Maintenance

During the school year, Graham's professional learning team set up a wiki to track its ongoing work and had a discussion board devoted to common language assessment. For each round of language assessment, partners recorded their student results on an Excel spreadsheet. Representatives from the learning team had a series of meetings with the district's assessment and technology committees to set up a more permanent management plan and iron out security details. Constructing common language assessment was carefully documented, and once it was finalized at Graham, the team wanted its process to be the prototype for the district.

Having selected their rubrics and language development benchmarks, the professional learning team spent time establishing inter-rater reliability; it realized the importance of maintaining consistency in interpreting student oral samples. The training on inter-rater agreement, led by the project's advisor, occurred on a district institute day; representative teachers from each school were invited. The team members were thrilled to reach a 90 percent agreement rate across all grades and attributed it, in part, to their ongoing participation in such a collaborative venture. Understanding this activity had to be repeated for every round of common assessment did not deter the team, since the members felt it was an enriching professional development experience that invited deep conversations about teaching and learning.

At the end of the academic year, the professional learning team finalized its common language assessments and celebrated its accomplishments. By adding common language assessment data to the profiles of English learners, Graham School created a comprehensive and inclusive assessment system that was sensitive to the individual needs of the students and contributed to school accountability. The stakeholders informed throughout the year of the work of the team came to extend congratulations, support the school, and applaud its efforts to further fair and meaningful assessment practices for its English learners.

Questions for Phase V: Maintenance

Approaching the last phase of construction, there are issues surrounding how to maintain the technical qualities of the common language assessment and ensure that the data remain meaningful to teachers and other stakeholders over time. The maintenance phase is an all school or district effort to institutionalize common language assessment that requires ongoing leadership, commitment, and support. Thus, it serves as one of advocacy for the construction process and the viability of common language assessment, especially for language learners.

Questions for Professional Learning Teams

A. **Management and Storage of Data From Common Language Assessment**

1. What constitutes a body of evidence, and can we consider language portfolios?

2. What is the role of technology in data storage and management?

3. What policies are in place for data input, protection, management, and retrieval?

4. What are the built-in provisions to evaluate construction, data management, and quality control each year?

B. **Issues of Reliability and Validity**

1. Does the common language assessment measure what it is intended to, are the results defensible, and is it operating within a valid system?

2. To what extent is there reliability of scoring (inter-rater agreement) for interpreting student work produced from the common language assessment, and how is it maintained over time?

3. How is continuity of common language assessment ensured from year to year?

4. How do results from common language assessment help confirm or predict the language proficiency of language learners?

C. **Maintenance of a Viable Language Assessment System**

1. What are the components of a language-centered assessment system inclusive of language learners?

2. How does a language-centered assessment system support high-quality language learning?

3. How might professional learning teams explore educational research to enhance the system?

4. What is the vision for the future of common language assessment for language learners?

Management and Storage of Data

Common language assessment is versatile in that it has multiple purposes and applications. If the data are to be used for local accountability purposes and complement large-scale state assessment, then it is important to establish a data management system to track students over time. It is the next logical step in the construction process that results in maintaining the status of common language assessment in a school or district, ensuring its vitality, and having clear evidence for making local decisions.

According to Kathyrn Lindholm-Leary and Gary Hargett (2007), data management is an integral component of an infrastructure in which:

- Assessment is aligned with standards and program goals
- Assessment is implemented consistently and systematically
- Assessment results are interpreted in a professional development series for teachers and school leaders
- Assessment results are disseminated to stakeholders
- A budget (and time) have been allocated to conduct such activities

When working with language learners, remember that additional data are necessary to capture a full profile of the students. There must be available and ample space (digital and physical) to record and maintain historical, demographic, language proficiency, and academic achievement data. Additionally, schools with dual language students require dual entries to represent ongoing performance of students in two languages.

Multiple Measures

Educators agree that any important educational decision should be based on multiple measures and a body of evidence that has been accrued over time. Sue Brookhart (2009) offers three distinct ways to define multiple measures—measures of different constructs (for example, reading and writing), different measures of the same construct (for example, an informal reading inventory and a multiple-choice reading test), and multiple opportunities to pass the same measure (for example, a high school graduation test).

Jan Chappuis, Stephen Chappuis, and Rick Stiggins (2009) assert that "the use of multiple measures does not, by itself, translate into high-quality evidence" (p. 15). The following criteria, which these assessment experts argue lead to quality assessment in general, have been stressed throughout this book in regard to language learners in particular:

- A specified purpose
- Clear learning targets
- A sound assessment design
- Effective communication of the results
- Student involvement in the assessment process (Stiggins, Arter, Chappuis, & Chappuis, 2006)

Multiple measures imply gathering information over an extended time span. Schools and districts have little control over the timeframe for state-required assessment; however, we can introduce other measures to gain more immediate and useful information. Table 6.1 (page 136) is a guide for determining the language-centered data sources that contribute to a management system for English learners that includes provision for measures in English and the students' other language.

Once the professional learning team has agreed on the sources of data entries, the next step is to name the specific measures and then create a master schedule. Activity 6.4, A Data Management Plan for English Learners (page 150 and online), is a template that duplicates table 6.1 (page 136). Use it to supply the names of measures, languages, collection windows, and persons responsible for inputting the results. A data coach or a consultant well-versed in assessment should assist in determining the means for entering data into the system. Finally, publish a data dictionary for all school personnel to better understand the scores, terms, and codes for each entry field.

With the pendulum swinging away from an exclusive reliance on standardized test data, schools and districts are again advocating for student portfolios as a vehicle for supporting high-quality learning (Darling-Hammond, 2010). Student portfolios may be viewed as bodies of evidence to be collected, interpreted, reported, and maintained over time.

Language Portfolios as Bodies of Evidence

Student portfolios may be exclusively built around common language assessment tasks and projects or in conjunction with other forms of assessment data. If the primary purpose is local accountability, then the same care that goes into ensuring the reliability and validity of each instructional assessment task must be extended to portfolios as a whole (Gottlieb, 1995). By amassing a variety of assessment tools in a showcase portfolio, a collection of students' prized work, teachers gain a comprehensive view of student performance (Rothenberg & Fisher, 2007). A pivotal portfolio, an organized, systematic collection of student work that provides authentic evidence of student learning over time, may also house common language assessments (Gottlieb & Nguyen, 2007).

Pivotal language portfolios are sensitive to the goals of local language education programs. Therefore, the portfolios of students in dual language classrooms, characterized by instruction in two languages, are distinct from those of students whose instruction is solely in English. To maximize their viability and usefulness for students, teachers, and administrators, portfolios that center on students' language development should have the following features:

- Representation of students' original work
- Evidence of students' language development in listening, speaking, reading, and/or writing
- Ample language assessments whose results are useful to multiple stakeholders, including students, family members, and teachers
- Internal reliability that shows consistency from language task to language task and comparability from year to year
- Internal validity that expresses the language education program's mission, goals, and student learning targets
- Provision of a rich portrait of a student's language learning

Table 6.1: Potential Data Sources for English Learners in a Management System

Potential Data Sources	In English	In Languages Other Than English	Collection Window
Demographic Information	✓		Upon entry in a state or school district
Educational History	✓		Upon entry in a school district
Language Proficiency Screeners	✓	✓	Upon entry in a state or school district
State English Language Proficiency Test	✓		Annually (K–12)
State Academic Achievement Tests	✓		Annually (3–12)
Interim Assessment for English Language Proficiency	✓		On a semester to quarterly basis
Common Language Assessment 1	✓	✓	
Common Language Assessment 2	✓	✓	
Common Language Assessment 3	✓	✓	
Student Language Portfolio	✓	✓	Ongoing

- Enough entries to have utility for local accountability; that is, the portfolio as a whole answers questions about the language education program, both internally within a school or district and externally to other stakeholders (Gottlieb & Nguyen, 2007)

Table 6.2 suggests a comprehensive portfolio for language development and special projects for language learners. School- and districtwide projects allow for student creativity and ingenuity by integrating content areas around a theme or conducting original research. There is also provision for fine arts, technology, and community service, in order to produce a well-rounded, educated individual who has demonstrated college and career readiness through multiple venues.

Table 6.2: Possible Common Assessment Entries in Language Portfolios

Language Development Across Language Domains	Evidence	
	L2	L1
Common Listening Tasks		
Common Speaking Tasks		
Common Reading Tasks		
Common Writing Tasks		
Common Integrated Language Tasks		
School or Districtwide Projects		
Community or School Service Projects		
Technology Projects		
Fine Arts or Integrated Projects		

A portfolio is an ideal archive for students to maintain data on their preset language goals over an academic year, but it can also be a logistical challenge. Using Activity 6.5, Considerations for Use of Evidence From Student Language Portfolios (page 151 and online), try experimenting with maintaining student portfolios for common language assessment.

Now that we have identified a body of evidence from common language assessment, we address storage capabilities and the role of technology in data maintenance.

The Role of Technology in Data Storage and Management

Information technology plays an increasing role in school life as educators come to rely on computers and other data-driven devices within the school environment. A national report issued by the Institute of Education Sciences highlights some of the important advances in the availability and use of technology in K–12 public schools. According to the findings from this survey, as of fall 2008:

- An estimated 100 percent of public schools have one or more instructional computers with Internet access
- 39 percent of public schools report having a wireless network
- About 33 percent of public schools have full-time staff devoted to technological support or integration
- 87 percent of public schools use their district network or the Internet to provide standardized test results to teachers
- 72 percent of public schools engage in online student assessment
- 85 percent of public schools use data from their network to inform instructional planning at the school level (Gray, Thomas, Lewis, & Tice, 2010)

These statistics suggest that schools are well positioned to use technology—in particular, computers—to inform stakeholders, store data, and use archived information for school and district improvement, strategic planning, or local accountability. In addition, the recent emergence of national consortia to develop computer adaptive and computer-driven content assessments in response to the Common Core State Standards is pushing schools and districts to become technology savvy. A rich and comprehensive profile of students emerges from data warehouses that contain students' demographic and historical information along with data from common language assessment, interim measures, and standardized tests.

Evaluating Construction, Data Management, and Quality Control

Planning, designing, and constructing language tasks and projects require a deliberate and thoughtful process. So too, does the treatment of assessment data. A system of checks and balances must be in place to maximize the usability of information for stakeholders. Once a year, an independent team, perhaps with representatives from each school in the district, should review procedures and policies to determine the fidelity of gathering, analyzing, recording, and maintaining data from common language assessment.

Quality control is critical and can extend beyond the maintenance phase if data from common language assessments are part of local accountability. Depending on the size of the district and, ultimately, the use of the data, evaluation should accompany each phase of common language assessment. The checklists in chapters 2–6 may serve as a starting point for learning teams to devise an overall evaluation plan for each phase of common language assessment. To understand the overall impact of common language assessment on teaching and learning, an evaluation plan should be incorporated into the last building block, the maintenance phase. School or district administrations should take this opportunity to decide whether to move forward with an independent evaluation or to conduct an internal audit or self-evaluation. Use

Activity 6.6, Evaluating the Common Language Assessment Project (page 152 and online), to help make that determination.

Now that constructing and implementing common language assessment is justifiable and useful to multiple stakeholders, it is important to show that the language tasks are psychometrically sound—that is, that there are proven reliabilities and validities. Determining the reliability and validity of common language assessment is a precursor to being able to make sound data-driven decisions.

Issues of Reliability and Validity

Why should the technical qualities of common language assessment even be under discussion in a book primarily geared to professional learning teams, not test developers? One reason for examining reliability and validity is to establish confidence in the results that are disseminated across the educational community. In addition, having trustworthy data puts common language assessment on a comparable footing as standardized test data.

Validity of Common Language Tasks

Validity, simply stated, is determining the extent to which a measure is truly representative of its claims; that is, does its purpose match how the results are used? In a traditional sense, validity is the degree of evidence that supports inferences from test scores (Messick, 1988). However, recently, the notion of validity has expanded to include argumentation for the interpretation of test scores (Kane, 1992), a principled framework to organize test evidence (Mislevy, Steinberg, & Almond, 1999), and the different sources of evidence collected before and after test administration (Weir, 2005).

Systemic validity for common language assessment emerges from the evidence accrued throughout the five-phase construction process. In a sense, validity is the superstructure on which assessment rests. By adhering to the checklists for each phase of common assessment, schools and districts can begin to establish evidence for systemic validity.

Reliability, or consistency, is another important quality of assessment. Common language assessment that is performance-based and woven into classroom practices involves educators examining the quality of student work and coming to agreement on scoring procedures. The following section describes the process for reaching consensus on interpreting student work using a uniform set of criteria.

Inter-Rater Reliability

Inter-rater agreement among teachers scoring performance assessment is critical to establishing and maintaining reliability; it is also a terrific opportunity for job-embedded professional development. Expanding on the previous chapter, here are some easy steps for professional learning teams to reach inter-rater agreement on student language samples in speaking or writing:

Select a group leader familiar with the procedure.

1. Have the anchor papers and the range-finder papers for each language task or project in hand or posted within easy reach.

2. Review and discuss the criteria of the rubric for each performance level (and dimension, if an analytic scale is used).

3. Distribute ten papers of students' writing samples or listen to tapes of oral samples with student names replaced by a numerical code or student ID, and independently, score the language samples against the rubric.

4. Determine initial reliability by plotting the exact and adjacent scores to see how many (what percentage) are in agreement or by attaching sticky notes to the anchor papers and calculating the percentage.

5. Debrief the practice exercise as a whole group—have participants provide evidence and justification of the choices they make. . . until consensus of the score is reached.

6. Form partners; distribute a new set of ten papers or oral language samples and have each person keep a separate rating or score, referring to the descriptors in the rubric, performance definitions of the levels of language proficiency, and anchor papers, as necessary.

Using a reliability graph, as shown in figure 6.1, have each partner plot the scores or ratings; together, the pair determines inter-rater agreement for exact scores and adjacent scores. Adjacent scores are one score point above or below an assigned one; for example, on a five-point rubric, if the assigned score is 3, it is the exact score if matched to that of the raters. In this case, 2 and 4 are adjacent scores and 1 and 5, being two score points away from the assigned one, are discrepant scores.

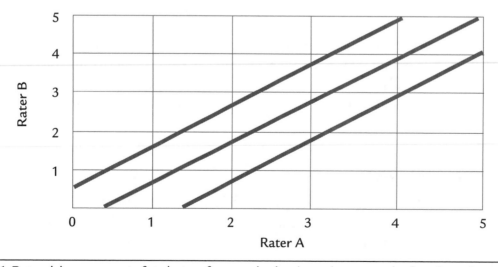

Figure 6.1: Determining agreement of student performance levels using an inter-rater plot for a five-point scale or rubric.

If inter-rater agreement is not in an acceptable range (from 80 to 90 percent), spend time reviewing the most troubling language samples (those with discrepant scores) until the group reaches consensus in regard to an assigned score or performance level.

Have the group leader determine the overall inter-rater reliability for the language task. If the performance extends across more than one grade, then determine inter-rater reliability for each grade and aggregate the scores for the entire sample of students.

Keep a record of the number of samples scored, by language task, grade, date, and the final inter-rater score.

Repeat the process every time you collect original student samples from common language assessment tasks that are used for accountability purposes. Figure 6.1 is set for two raters (A and B) to plot their scores from student language samples. If there is exact agreement, the score point falls in the center diagonal. That is, if both raters assign a 4, then the score point marks 4 on the vertical axis and 4 on the horizontal one. The two lines drawn parallel to the center diagonal define the area that represents a discrepancy of one score point or level. So, if rater A gives a holistic score of 3 and rater B gives a 2, their combined score point is on the lower diagonal; if the reverse happens, and rater A assigns a 2 and rater B a 3, the score point appears on the upper diagonal.

Generally, when establishing inter-rater reliability, we report both exact scores and adjacent scores. Use Activity 6.7, Determining Inter-Rater Agreement on Student Language Samples (page 154 and online), as a template for recording and maintaining inter-rater agreement for common assessment tasks.

In calculating inter-rater reliability, there are no right or wrong scores per se; what is important is that the raters agree on how they approach and assign scores so that there is consistency in applying the rubric's criteria.

Use of Results

Common language assessment provides timely results for teachers to make instructional decisions and for students to receive descriptive feedback. As shown in table 6.1 (page 136), there are several sources of state and local language data to balance a language learner's portfolio. When results from common language assessment are stored in a central location on a school or district server, teachers and administrators can readily see how results help confirm students' language proficiency from other data sources, namely, interim assessments and state accountability measures. Using Activity 6.8, Maintaining Data Sources for English Learners Over Time (page 155 and online), note the specific measures used in your school or district; then identify the scores on language measures to maintain over the course of a student's school career.

Let's not forget the benefits of using results from common language assessment for English learners with potential or identified learning disabilities. If these students have been included in all phases of constructing common language assessment, then the results should be valid indicators of what these students can do in one or two languages. These data have important implications for those students who may be considered for Tier 2 (intensive supplemental instruction) or Tier 3 (intensive individual instruction) within a response to intervention framework. As advocates for English learners, we need to dispel the common misconception that English learners with disabilities cannot benefit from instruction and assessment in two languages (Hamayan, Marler, Sanchez-Lopez, & Damico, 2007). Interestingly, research indicates that even children with severe language impairments have the capacity to become bilingual and that working in their native language promotes second language development (Genesee et al., 2004).

Thinking about the heterogeneity of the growing population of language learners in our schools and the amount of available data in today's world, our final step in this building block is putting together a sustainable structure.

Maintenance of a Viable Language Assessment System

Having thoughtfully deliberated on each building block in the construction process, we now integrate the measures that constitute common language assessment into a viable system. A valid assessment system geared to language learners begins with clear, high-quality standards and their close alignment with assessments. Standards are the footing for curriculum and instruction, while assessments provide the data on student performance (Wolf, Herman, & Dietel, 2010). Figure 6.2 is an example of such a system, in which the interplay between language proficiency and academic achievement is clearly visible.

In an ideal world, one assessment system should represent each and every student fairly. In reality, there are assessment systems designed for English learners and others for students with disabilities, including English learners with disabilities; somehow they are to operate within the overall assessment system for the general school population.

Educational Systems That Support High-Quality Learning

The forward thinking of Linda Darling-Hammond (2010) speaks to assessment systems that support high-quality learning for all students. In these systems, stakeholders have a keen awareness of learning expectations, of how to support learning, and of how to maintain information from learning in a longitudinal data system. These systems address:

- The depth and breadth of standards and curriculum
- The characteristics and needs of all students
- Challenging content on which students receive feedback on a regular basis
- Multiple forms of assessment
- Teachers who partake in scoring student work based on shared learning targets

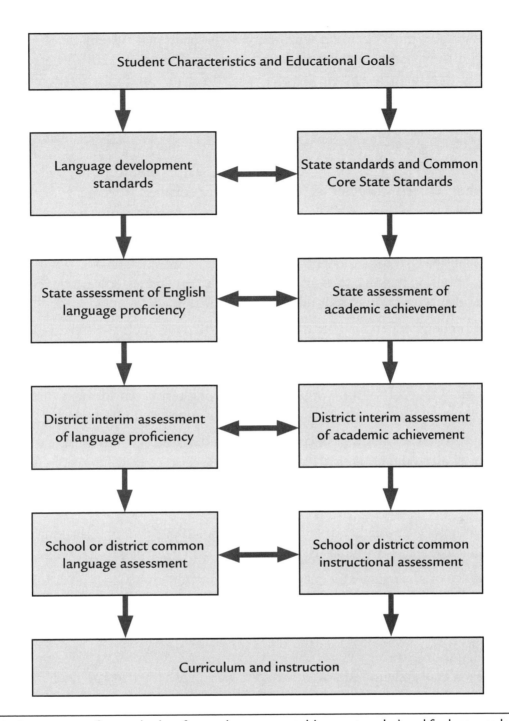

Figure 6.2: Components of a standards-referenced, assessment-driven system designed for language learners.

Additionally, Darling-Hammond (2010) states that "high achieving systems seek to implement their standards with assessments that measure performance in authentic ways and with intensive teacher engagement throughout the assessment process, as teachers work with others to develop, review, score, and use the results of assessments. Comparability in scoring is achieved through the use of standardized rubrics, as well as training" (p. 4). Professional learning teams can spearhead this effort.

Assessment systems must function within greater educational systems. Examining school change through the lens of English learners, Rosa Horwitz et al. (2009) noted a series of shared contextual features and promising practices of urban school districts that have undergone academic improvement of this subgroup of students since 2002. These features, which characterize systemic comprehensive reform efforts, include:

- A shared vision for reform in which districts capitalize on new accountability demands for English learners as an opportunity to develop, communicate, and rally support behind a unified vision for districtwide instructional improvement

- School and district leadership who advocate on behalf of English learners and support teachers in improving instruction and services for their students

- Recognition that directors of language programs are valuable contributors to central-office decision making, thus giving them authority and empowerment comparable to other district personnel to establish policies and practices

- Comprehensive planning for districtwide initiatives, such as literacy programs, that includes special attention for English learners and provision of resources to support their academic language development

- Implementation of reforms approached as a long-term commitment that is accompanied by clear guidance, tools, and oversight from the central office

- A shift to a school culture of collaboration and shared accountability for the achievement of all students

- Employment of strategic school staffing to maximize teaching and learning for English learners and improve consistency of instruction

- Provision of high-quality, relevant, and sustained professional development targeted to all stakeholders working with or serving English learners

- Reliance on the use of student data as a cornerstone for school or district reform by all stakeholders

- Reallocation of existing resources and strategic use of funds earmarked for English learners

These key features of systemic educational reform for English learners can readily be evaluated in reference to common language assessment; Activity 6.9, Maintaining a Vision of Excellence for English Learners (page 156 and online), converts these positive elements of systemic reform for English learners into a rating scale.

Without ongoing research centered on seeking viable solutions to issues challenging the education of English learners, we will not be able to make advancements in serving this growing student population.

Enhancing Instructional Assessment Systems for English Learners Through Educational Research

Research agendas and policy documents have been issued throughout the years that specifically address issues related to the education of English learners (for example, August & Hakuta, 1997), but there has been little action on these sets of recommendations. Recently, Mikyung Kim Wolf, Joan Herman, and Ronald Dietel (2010) suggested an agenda that examines issues related to:

- Policies and their impact on English learners
- Expansion of the research base on academic language
- Validity of the uses of English language proficiency assessments
- Guidelines for constructing fair tests
- Proven accommodations to content tests to bolster student achievement
- Opportunities for English learners to learn

The field of language education currently has the theoretical and research base that supports language as a resource paradigm (Escamilla & Hopewell, 2010). However, there still remains much room for the construction of reliable and valid assessments in English and other languages that measure language targets, referenced to standards, and are designed for language learners.

The Future of Common Language Assessment for Language Learners

The student demographics of today and future generations cannot be overlooked. The continued exponential increase in the numbers and needs of English learners in our schools is cause for reframing how we educate our youth. We must remain steadfast in the conviction that, irrespective of federal mandates, common language assessment, built by consensus at a school, district, or language program level, can have a direct impact on the meaning of instruction and how we function as educators. By having comprehensive profiles of our students' language proficiency created from sound data, we will be able to forge ahead and make continuous improvements in how we teach and how our students learn.

The synergy from collaboration among teachers and administrators sparks creativity in planning, constructing, refining, and even reconfiguring common language assessment. Assessment data and evidence for language learning crafted and contextualized for specific groups and subgroups of students are deeply embedded in educational reform efforts.

Technology plays an increasing role in our daily lives, and we can only begin to imagine how it will become totally integrated into schooling of the future. Assessment and accountability will cease to be an annual event of data collection and will become an internally motivated, ever-present process that engages and energizes stakeholders. But ultimately, it is caring humans, not machines, who will use those data to ensure that the students of tomorrow will indeed have ample opportunities to prosper in our multicultural, global society.

Recap of the Maintenance Phase

Construction may be nearing completion, but we must always consider care and maintenance, so that common language assessment will reap benefits for years to come. In this phase, we center our attention on ensuring that reliable and valid sources of common language assessment have provided the data for decision making. Here is a summary of the major steps in this phase:

1. Accrue a defensible body of evidence from common language assessment.
2. Make provision for storage of student historical, demographic, and assessment data.
3. Provide arguments for and evidence that common language assessments are reliable and valid for language learners.
4. Build inter-rater agreement of student work samples from performance assessment into ongoing professional development of teachers working with language learners.
5. Finalize and maintain a language-centered assessment system that is comprehensive, fair, valid, practical, and defensible for language learners.

It has been a long, yet rewarding journey to develop common language assessment. You have spent a tremendous amount of time and energy gathering input from multiple stakeholders. Let's place our last building block into position.

Building Blocks

A district, program, or school's drive for educational excellence may be a compelling reason for establishing and maintaining a database of local and state measures for its language learners. In it, we retain data unique to English learners as part of an overall management system, so that educators of language learners have deep insights into students' language development. Data from common language assessment accumulated purposively and systemically hold promise for demonstrating students' language growth over time. As we moved through the phases of construction, from planning to designing to refining to inspecting and, finally, to maintaining, we have accumulated invaluable knowledge of how to work within a community of learners and how, collectively, educators can make a difference in the lives of the students they serve. By carefully documenting each building block of common language assessment, we create a strong inclusionary, enduring, and replicable process that honors students, teachers, and school leaders.

Activity 6.1
Last Chance!

Last chance! Propose any remaining questions for each of the three topics pertaining to the maintenance phase.

A. Management and Storage of Data From Common Language Assessment

B. Issues of Reliability and Validity

C. Maintenance of a Viable Language Assessment System

Activity 6.2
Checklist for Phase V: Maintenance

Modify this checklist based on the comments and questions related to the topics in Activity 6.1 (page 147) and use it, along with other checklists, in formative or summative evaluation of the common language assessment project.

A. Management and Storage of Data From Common Language Assessment

☐ Assemble a body of evidence from common language assessment.

☐ Decide the role of technology in data storage and management.

☐ Set policies for data input, protection, management, and retrieval.

☐ Include provisions to evaluate construction, data management, and quality control every year.

B. Issues of Reliability and Validity

☐ Document the validity of common language assessment as well as the assessment system in which it is operating.

☐ Maintain consistency of scoring (inter-rater agreement) for language production and reliability in interpreting student work.

☐ Ensure continuity of common language assessment data from year to year.

☐ Use other language proficiency data to corroborate or refute the results from common language assessment.

C. Maintenance of a Viable Language Assessment System

☐ Verify that the components of an instructional assessment system are designed for language learners, in particular, English learners.

☐ Make sure that the language-centered assessment system supports high-quality language learning.

☐ Explore how educational research might enhance the assessment system.

☐ Formulate a vision of the future of assessment for language learners based on the construction of common language assessment.

Activity 6.3
People and Timeline for Phase V: Maintenance

What will it take to manage and maintain the common language assessment system that you have built?

Activities and Decisions	Beginning and Ending Dates	Person(s) Responsible
A. Management and Storage of Data From Common Language Assessment		
A.1		
A.2		
A.3		
A.4		
B. Issues of Reliability and Validity		
B.1		
B.2		
B.3		
B.4		
C. Maintenance of a Viable Language Assessment System		
C.1		
C.2		
C.3		
C.4		

Activity 6.4
A Data Management Plan for English Learners

Use this table as a template for considering the data sources to be maintained over time. Take time to spell out the specifics of a data management plan around language assessment of English and other languages.

Potential Data Sources	In English	In Languages Other Than English	Collection Window
Demographic Information			
Educational History			
Language Proficiency Screeners			
State English Language Proficiency Test			
State Academic Achievement Tests			
Interim Assessment for English Language Proficiency			
Interim Assessment for Language Proficiency in Other Languages			
Common Language Assessment for English Language Proficiency			
Common Language Assessment for Language Proficiency in Other Languages			
Student Language Portfolio			

Activity 6.5
Considerations for Use of Evidence From Student Language Portfolios

Break up into small groups and jigsaw, a process in which each group is assigned a couple of questions drawn from the following list, after which the whole group reunites and shares responses.

1. Which language domain, language tasks, or school projects do you wish to begin to accrue evidence?

2. How many entries from common language assessment and other data do you plan to gather throughout the academic year?

3. Are the entries to be equally spaced in time (for example, monthly), and if so, when do you anticipate data collection?

4. How might you use technology to store entries or create and maintain a digital portfolio (for example, for speaking or writing)?

5. How might student self-assessment or reflection be built into a language portfolio?

6. Will language portfolios contribute to the grading of language learners? If so, how?

7. Which entries count for local accountability, and how much does each entry count? That is, are some entries weighted more than others? Which ones, and why?

8. Has a procedure been established for reviewing the students' portfolios and assigning an overall language proficiency score?

9. Is there a data management system in place? If so, how and how often might the data for the portfolios be entered?

Activity 6.6
Evaluating the Common Language Assessment Project

Here are three easy ways that schools or districts may choose to evaluate their common language assessment project.

Evaluation Option 1: Devise a goal for each of the five building blocks—planning, design, refinement, inspection, and maintenance. Then, for each goal, select the types of evidence reflective of the goal. Next, based on the evidence, determine the extent to which the goal has been accomplished in deciles (percent by tens) or descriptors, such as *not as much as expected*, *met our expectations*, or *exceeded our expectations*. Finally, explain the strengths of the project and how it might be improved in the future. The following table displays these major elements for the evaluation.

Construction Phase	Goal	Types of Evidence	Extent of Accomplishment (in % or by descriptors)
Planning			
Design			
Refinement			
Inspection			
Maintenance			

Evaluation Option 2: Select the three major topics for each phase of construction, displayed in chapters 2 through 6. Then convert the checklist for each topic into a rating scale to express the extent to which that aspect of construction has been accomplished not at all, partially, or completely.

A starting point for this evaluation option may be found in the following sample taken from Phase II: Design.

Topic A: Overall Design			
The purposes for common language assessment have been determined.	**Has not been accomplished 1**	**Has been partially accomplished 2**	**Has been completely accomplished 3**
Evidence of Accomplishment:			

Topic B: Examination and Selection of Standards			
Grade levels, languages, standards, and language domains have been identified.	**Has not been accomplished 1**	**Has been partially accomplished 2**	**Has been completely accomplished 3**
Evidence of Accomplishment:			

Topic C: Common Language Tasks			
Language goals identify long-term expectations, language targets focus on expectations for units of instruction, and language objectives differentiate language tasks by language proficiency levels.	**Has not been accomplished 1**	**Has been partially accomplished 2**	**Has been completely accomplished 3**
Evidence of Accomplishment:			

Evaluation Option 3: Combine the two methodologies for evaluation. Use Option 2 on a formative basis at the completion of each building block, and use Option 1 as a summative evaluation tool at the close of the entire project.

Activity 6.7
Determining Inter-Rater Agreement on Student Language Samples

Duplicate this activity to use in determining inter-rater agreement on a practice set of student samples. Working in pairs, Rater A and Rater B score the same student samples independently, and then each completes the designated column. Reach a percent agreement based on the number of exact score matches and another on those scores discrepant by 1 (+1 or -1).

Language Task: _____

Grade: _____

Date: _____

Student Sample #	Rater A Score	Rater B Score	Exact Score	Discrepancy (+1, -1)
1.				
2.				
3.				
4.				
5.				
6.				
7.				
8.				
9.				
10.				
Percent Agreement on Exact Score:				
Percent Agreement on Scores Discrepant by + or -1:				

Activity 6.8
Maintaining Data Sources for English Learners Over Time

Here is a way to display different forms of assessment and data for English learners throughout a school year; unlike the tables in the chapter, it includes provision for both language and achievement data. Use this activity as a starting point for thinking about the usefulness of data from year to year. Adapt this table to fit the needs of individual schools and districts, and review the data on an annual basis.

Student Background and Historical Data							
Date	Language Proficiency Measures	L1 Score	L2 (English) Score	Date	Academic Achievement Measures	L1 Score	L2 Score
	State ELP Test: Composite				State English Language Arts/ Reading Test		
	State ELP Test: Oral Language				State Mathematics Test		
	State ELP Test: Literacy				State Science Test		
	State ELP Test: Comprehension				District Interim Content Assessment		
	Interim Language Assessment				District Interim Content Assessment		
	Common Language Assessment				Common Content Assessment		
	Common Language Assessment				Common Content Assessment		
	Common Language Assessment				Common Content Assessment		
	Overall Language Proficiency Portfolio				Overall Achievement Portfolio		

Common Language Assessment for English Learners © 2012 Solution Tree Press · solution-tree.com
Visit **go.solution-tree.com/ELL** to download this page.

Activity 6.9
Maintaining a Vision of Excellence for English Learners

The findings from the Horwitz et al., 2009, study have been converted into a rating scale. Evaluate the extent to which initiatives and reforms have been institutionalized for English learners in your setting.

Mark the column that best describes the amount of evidence you have to judge each promising practice. You may wish to offer concrete examples of evidence of each practice.

Promising Practices for Language Learners	Not Evident	Somewhat Evident	Fully Evident
1. A shared vision for educational reform			
2. Support and advocacy by school and district leadership			
3. Authority and empowerment of directors of language education programs to establish policies and practices			
4. Comprehensive planning for districtwide initiatives and resources			
5. Clear guidance, tools, and oversight from the central office for district reforms			
6. A culture of collaboration and shared accountability for the achievement of all students			
7. Strategic school staffing to maximize teaching and learning and improve consistency of instruction			
8. High-quality, relevant, and sustained professional development targeted to all stakeholders			
9. Use of student data as a cornerstone for school or district reform			
10. Reallocation of existing resources and strategic use of funds			

Adapted from Succeeding With English Language Learners: Lessons From the Great City Schools (2009), *by Amanda Rose Horwitz, Gabriela Uro, Ricki Price-Baugh, Candace Simon, Renata Uzzell, Sharon Lewis et al. Washington, DC: Council of the Great City Schools.*

Glossary

academic achievement tests. Measurement of the skills and knowledge associated with content-area curriculum.

academic language. The language required to successfully negotiate school, which includes the acquisition of new and deeper understandings of content related to curriculum, communication of those understandings to others, and effective participation in the classroom environment. These understandings revolve around specific aspects of language registers (social and academic), language structures (vocabulary, grammar, and discourse), and language functions.

adjacent scores. One score point above or below an assigned one in a scale; for example, on a five-point rubric, if the assigned score is 3, then 2 and 4 would be considered adjacent scores.

analytic scales. Rubrics, often in the form of matrices, with sets of criteria for each of several traits or dimensions for each score point.

anchor papers. Selected student samples that represent the mid-range of a performance level.

anecdotal notes. Comments on the behaviors or skills of individual students that are maintained by teachers.

assessment. The gathering of information over time from multiple sources that, when analyzed and reported, communicates evidence of student performance.

balanced bilinguals. Persons who have relatively the same levels of proficiency in two languages.

benchmarks. Preset performance or assessment targets; points on a scale that delineate attainable goals for students.

benchmark tests. Measures administered at a predetermined time in the instructional cycle or point on the learning continuum; specified tests given multiple times a year to determine if students are on the trajectory toward meeting accountability targets.

biliteracy. The development of reading and writing skills in two languages.

checklists. Dichotomous scales with traits marked as either present or absent that do not include judgment of quality.

cognitive functions. Mental processes involved in learning.

Common Core State Standards or **academic content standards.** The skills and knowledge descriptive of student expectations, minimally in English language arts, mathematics, and literacy in history/social studies, science, and technical subjects, at each grade.

common instructional assessment. A mutually agreed-upon set of instructionally embedded measures or uniform procedures that involve planning, collecting, interpreting, and reporting data, generally from the content areas, across multiple classrooms.

common language assessment. A type of common instructional assessment; mutually agreed-upon language measures or language tasks embedded in instruction that involve uniform procedures for collecting, analyzing, and interpreting language data across multiple classrooms.

constructed-response. Open-ended or performance assessments where students can organize and use their knowledge and skills, apply their learning, and engage in imagination, creativity, and originality in producing responses that are interpreted with performance criteria.

criterion-referenced measures. Assessment geared around established criteria, such as standards, for its development and reporting of results.

differentiation of instruction. The efforts of teachers to respond to the diversity and variance among learners to maximize their classroom learning experiences.

differentiation of language. Matching the linguistic complexity and vocabulary of written or oral discourse to the students' levels of English language proficiency to maximize their access to grade-level content; adapting instruction and assessment according to English learners' levels of English language proficiency.

discourse. The ways in which oral and written language are organized, such as in academic disciplines or specific genres.

discrepant scores. Generally, two or more score points above or below an assigned one; for example, on a five-point rubric, if the assigned score is 3, then 1 and 5 would be considered discrepant scores.

documentation forms. Means of recording (and reporting) student data based on instructional assessment tasks.

dual language education or two-way immersion programs. Enriched and additive learning environments that benefit two groups of students, such as English learners of one language integrated and learning side-by-side with their proficient English peers, with the overall goal of both groups of students becoming bilingual and biliterate, attaining grade-level achievement, and developing positive cross-cultural attitudes and competencies.

English learners. The subset of linguistically and culturally diverse students whose English language proficiency has not yet developed to a point where they can access academic content sufficiently to fully benefit from instruction in English.

evaluation. Making judgments based on the match between (educational) goals and their related body of evidence.

fidelity. Robustness in implementation of a procedure or program in order to maximize opportunities for replication.

formative information. Providing students timely, descriptive feedback on their progress and learning, while providing teachers ongoing feedback on their instruction.

genre. Text types of and within different disciplines.

heritage language learners. Third or fourth generation residents of a country, or indigenous peoples, who retain their original cultural identity, but have not maintained oral academic and written competencies in a language other than English.

holistic scales. Rubrics with sets of criteria that are written for each score point.

home language survey. A screening form, usually administered upon students' initial entry into a school district, that consists of a series of questions to determine whether students come from linguistically and culturally diverse backgrounds.

informal reading inventories. Individually administered, performance-based assessments of different aspects of reading, including vocabulary knowledge, comprehension, and fluency.

instructional assessment. The integration of instruction and assessment that occurs at the classroom level.

instructional assessment activities. Short-term probes during a lesson or a summary of learning at the close of a lesson.

instructional assessment projects. Several related tasks that scaffold over a unit of instruction that allow students to demonstrate their academic language and in-depth knowledge of a topic or theme.

instructional assessment tasks. Multistep or scaffolded activities that are a class period or two in length.

instructional supports. Available sensory, graphic, and interactive resources to assist students in constructing meaning from language and content.

interim assessment. Generally commercially produced tests that are administered at designated times throughout the school year with the intent of predicting student performance on annual high-stakes tests.

inter-rater agreement (or inter-rater reliability). The percentage of exact (and adjacent) agreement on the assignment of a score for a student's performance by two or more scorers; the process of reaching consensus on interpreting student work using a uniform set of criteria.

language domains. Listening, speaking, reading, and writing.

language functions. Linguistic processes required in conveying a message.

language goals. Projected language outcomes for language education programs or global curricular language expectations for English learners.

language objectives. Specific language outcomes for language lessons.

language proficiency. A person's competence in processing (through listening and reading) and using (through speaking and writing) language.

language proficiency standards. Descriptions of the language expectations for students that are marked by specified progressions or levels across the language development continuum.

language proficiency tests. Measures of listening, speaking, reading, and writing designed to demonstrate how English learners process and produce language.

language targets. Language expectations or outcomes for a language-centered curriculum designed for English learners.

levels of language proficiency. The stages along the pathway of language development.

long-term English learners. A subset of English learners who generally have received more than seven years of language support, but whose English language proficiency appears to have fossilized about midpoint along the second language acquisition continuum.

mechanical cloze. A type of reading comprehension measure whereby every nth (for example, every seventh) word is deleted from a passage and students are required to replace it based on the context of the discourse.

migrant students. Linguistically and culturally diverse students who have interrupted their formal education due to travels throughout the academic year dictated by parent or guardian employment in some form of temporary or seasonal agricultural-related work.

native language (L1). Students' primary home language and generally their first language acquired.

newcomers. Typically, older students who are recent arrivals usually within the previous five years, with little or no prior exposure to English.

norm-referenced measures. Tests in which student performance or scores are ranked against those of other students, distributed along a bell curve, and expressed in percentiles or stanines.

peer assessment. Targeted or descriptive feedback on student work from fellow students based on standards-referenced criteria.

performance assessment. Tasks or projects that produce original student work, which are often embedded in instruction and scored with a rubric.

performance criteria. Descriptors for guiding or interpreting student responses, work samples, or products.

pivotal portfolio. An organized, systematic collection of student work that provides authentic evidence of student learning over time.

professional learning teams. Groups of educators, including teachers and administrators, who meet, communicate, and collaborate on a regular basis to accomplish a common set of goals—in this case, to create instructional assessment for English learners.

project descriptors. Criteria that define the quality of a series of related instructional activities and tasks that allow students to explore a topic or theme in depth.

psychometric properties. The reliability and validity of tests or assessment measures.

range-finder papers. Selected samples of student work that fall between performance levels; for example, on a four-point rubric, a student's writing might be considered a 2+ or a 3-.

rating scales. A type of rubric in which traits, skills, strategies, or behaviors are assessed by their frequency of occurrence (how often) or quality (how well).

rational cloze. A type of reading comprehension measure whereby a syntactic structure (for example, all the prepositions) or word choice (such as all the adjectives) is systematically deleted from a passage and students are required to replace it based on the context of the discourse.

register. Features of language that vary according to the context and purpose of the communication (for example, the speech used when students talk to their peers versus that used when they speak to their principal).

reliability. Dependable data based on consistency in scoring and reporting.

response to intervention (RTI). An evidence-based, multitiered, problem-solving model, established with the Individuals with Disabilities Education Act (IDEA) of 2004, intended to provide high-quality instruction or intervention matched to student needs.

robustness. The rigor of a task or project; that is, its depth and breadth.

rubrics. Scoring guides or documentation forms with descriptive criteria used to interpret data or judge the quality of student work samples or products from performance assessment.

screening instruments. Measures used to make an overall, initial determination, such as whether students are eligible for specific services.

selected-response. Discrete-point assessments or tests with answers that are restricted to multiple-choice, true-false, or matching.

self-assessment. Students' use of performance criteria or descriptors to interpret their own work.

sequential bilinguals. Persons who acquire a second language after the foundation of their first language has been established.

showcase portfolio. A collection of students' prized or most accomplished work.

simultaneous bilinguals. Persons who are exposed to and are given opportunities to learn two languages from a very young age.

social language. The everyday and instructional registers used in interactions outside and inside school.

stakeholders. Persons involved in or impacted by educational decisions (from data from common assessment).

standard assessment. See common language assessment.

standardized tests. Measures that are administered without deviation from the script, uniformly scored, and whose results are interpreted in the identical manner.

students with interrupted formal education (SIFE). The subset of English learners, generally in grades four through high school, who have had inconsistent schooling experiences either in the United States or their native land.

summative evaluation. The systematic process of determining the effectiveness or worth of a project or educational program.

summative information. Data that are collected, analyzed, and reported at the culmination of a project, time period, or instructional assessment cycle; the "sum" of evidence gathered over time.

tallies. Marks or slashes denoting frequency of occurrence that are used as a means for documenting evidence of student performance.

task-specific rubric. Criteria for success of student performance descriptive of a particular task or project.

technical qualities. See psychometric properties.

think-aloud. A metacognitive strategy descriptive of the actions related to how information is processed and conveyed.

trend data. The accumulation of the same information collected from the identical source in the same way over three or more years.

two-way immersion. Language-learning environments in which English learners, alongside their proficient English peers, receive content and literacy instruction in English and a partner language.

validity. The state of being realistic and meaningful; a description of inferences drawn from data that are suitable for a measure's given purpose and audience.

References and Resources

Absolum, M., Flockton, L., Hattie, J., Hipkins, R., & Reid, I. (2008). *Directions for assessment in New Zealand: A strategy for developing students' assessment capabilities.* Wellington, New Zealand: Te Kete Ipurangi. Accessed at www.tki.org.nz/r /assessment/docs/danz.doc on July 12, 2009.

Adger, C. T., Snow, C. E., & Christian, D. (Eds.). (2002). *What teachers need to know about language.* Washington, DC: Center for Applied Linguistics/Delta Systems.

Agor, B. (Ed.). (2000). *Integrating the ESL standards into classroom practice: Grades 9–12.* Alexandria, VA: Teachers of English to Speakers of Other Languages.

Ainsworth, L., & Christinson, J. (1998). *Student-generated rubrics: An assessment model to help all students succeed.* Orangeburg, NY: Addison-Wesley.

Ainsworth, L., & Viegut, D. (2006). *Common formative assessments: How to connect standards-based instruction and assessment.* Thousand Oaks, CA: Corwin Press.

Ardovino, J., Hollingsworth, J., & Ybarra, S. (2000). *Multiple measures: Accurate ways to assess student achievement.* Thousand Oaks, CA: Corwin Press.

Arter, J., & McTighe, J. (2001). *Scoring rubrics in the classroom: Using performance criteria for assessing and improving student performance.* Thousand Oaks, CA: Corwin Press.

August, D., & Hakuta, K. (Eds.). (1997). *Improving schooling for language minority children: A research agenda.* Washington, DC: National Research Council.

August, D., & Shanahan, T. (Eds.). (2006). *Developing reading and writing in second language learners: Report of the National Literacy Panel on Language-Minority Children and Youth.* Mahwah, NJ: Erlbaum.

Bailey, A. L. (Ed.). (2007). *The language demands of school: Putting academic language to the test.* Princeton, NJ: Yale University Press.

Bailey, A. L., & Butler, F. A. (2002). *An evidentiary framework for operationalizing academic language for broad application to K–12 education: A design document.* Los Angeles: Center for the Study of Evaluation/National Center for Research on Evaluation, Standards, and Student Testing.

Bailey, A. L., & Heritage, M. (2008). *Formative assessment for literacy, grades K–6: Building reading and academic language skills across the curriculum.* Thousand Oaks, CA: Corwin Press.

Bernhardt, V. L. (1998). *Multiple measures* (Monograph No. 4). Alexandria, VA: Association for Supervision and Curriculum Development.

Black, P., & Wiliam, D. (1998). Inside the black box: Raising standards through classroom assessment. *Phi Delta Kappan, 80*(2), 139–148.

Brookhart, S. M. (2009). The many meanings of "multiple measures." *Educational Leadership, 67*(3), 6–12.

Brown, H. D. (2004). *Language assessment: Principles and classroom practices.* White Plains, NY: Pearson.

Brown, J. E., & Doolittle, J. (2008). *A cultural, linguistic, and ecological framework for response to intervention for English language learners.* Tempe, AZ: National Center for Culturally Responsive Educational Systems. Accessed at www.nccrest.org/Briefs /Framework_for_RTI.pdf on March 11, 2011.

Bryk, A. S., Sebring, P. B., Allensworth , E., Luppescu, S., & Easton, J. Q. (2010). *Organizing schools for improvement: Lessons from Chicago.* Chicago: University of Chicago Press.

Capps, R., Fix, M., Murray, J., Ost, J., Passel, J., & Herwantoro, S. (2005). *The new demography of America's schools: Immigration and the No Child Left Behind Act.* Washington, DC: Urban Institute.

Carr, J. F., & Harris, D. E. (2001). *Succeeding with standards: Linking curriculum, assessment, and action planning.* Alexandria, VA: Association for Supervision and Curriculum Development.

Carr, J., Sexton, U., & Lagunoff, R. (2006). *Making science accessible to English learners: A guide for teachers.* San Francisco: WestEd.

Center for Applied Linguistics. (2010). *Exemplary programs for newcomer English language learners at the secondary level.* Accessed at www.cal.org/projects/newcomer.html on March 11, 2011.

Chalhoub-Deville, M. (2008, April). *Standards-based assessment in the USA: Social and educational impact.* Presented at the ALTE 3rd International Conference, Cambridge, England.

Chamot, A. U., & O'Malley, J. M. (1994). *The CALLA handbook: Implementing the Cognitive Academic Language Learning Approach.* Reading, MA: Addison-Wesley.

Chapman, C., & King, R. (2005). *Differentiated assessment strategies: One tool doesn't fit all.* Thousand Oaks, CA: Corwin Press.

Chappuis, S., Chappuis, J., & Stiggins, R. (2009). The quest for quality. *Educational Leadership, 67*(3), 14–19.

Chevalier, C. M. (2008). *Tapestry for teachers of English language learners.* Accessed at www .tesol.org/s_tesol/cat_tapestry.asp?CID=1585&DID=8732 on March 11, 2011.

Cloud, N., Genesee, F., & Hamayan, E. (2000). *Dual language instruction: A handbook for enriched education.* Boston: Heinle & Heinle.

Coggins, D., Kravin, D., Coates, G. D., & Carroll, M. D. (2007). *English language learners in the mathematics classroom.* Thousand Oaks, CA: Corwin Press.

Coltrane, B. (2003). *Working with young English language learners: Some considerations.* Washington, DC: Center for Applied Linguistics. Accessed at www.cal.org /resources/digest/0301coltrane.html on March 11, 2011.

Common Core State Standards Initiative. (2010). *The standards: Mathematics.* Accessed at www.corestandards.org/the-standards/mathematics on March 11, 2011.

Cummins, J. (1981). The cross-lingual dimensions of language proficiency: Implications for bilingual education and the optimal age issue. *TESOL Quarterly, 14,* 175–185.

Cummins, J. (2000). *Language, power, and pedagogy: Bilingual children in the crossfire.* Clevedon, England: Multilingual Matters.

Darling-Hammond, L. (1996). The quiet revolution: Rethinking teacher development. *Educational Leadership, 53*(6), 4–10.

Darling-Hammond, L. (2010). *Performance counts: Assessment systems that support high-quality learning.* Washington, DC: Council of Chief State School Officers.

Davies Samway, K. (Ed.). (2000). *Integrating the ESL standards into classroom practice: Grades 3–5.* Alexandria, VA: Teachers of English to Speakers of Other Languages.

Drake, S. M. (2007). *Creating standards-based integrated curriculum: Aligning curriculum, content, assessment, and instruction.* Thousand Oaks, CA: Corwin Press.

DuFour, R. (2004). What is a professional learning community? *Educational Leadership, 61*(8), 6–11.

DuFour, R., DuFour, R., Eaker, R., & Karhanek, G. (2004). *Whatever it takes: How professional learning communities respond when kids don't learn.* Bloomington, IN: Solution Tree Press.

DuFour, R., DuFour, R., Eaker, R., & Many, T. (2006). *Learning by doing: A handbook for professional learning communities at work.* Bloomington, IN: Solution Tree Press.

Echevarria, J., Vogt, M. E., & Short, D. J. (2008). *Making content comprehensible for English learners: The SIOP model* (3rd ed.). Boston: Allyn & Bacon.

Egbert, J. L., & Ernst-Slavit, G. (2010). *Access to academics: Planning instruction for K–12 classrooms with ELLs.* Boston: Pearson Education.

Escamilla, K., & Hopewell, S. (2010). Transitions to biliteracy: Creating positive academic trajectories for emerging bilinguals in the United States. In J. Petrovic (Ed.), *International perspectives on bilingual education: Policy, practice, controversy* (pp. 65–89). Charlotte, NC: Information Age.

Farr, B. P., & Trumbull, E. (1997). *Assessment alternatives for diverse classrooms.* Norwood, MA: Christopher-Gordon.

Fatham, A. K., & Crowther, D. T. (Eds.). (2006). *Science for English language learners: K–12 classroom strategies.* Arlington, VA: National Science Teachers Association.

Fogarty, R., & Pete, B. (2009/2010). Professional learning 101: A syllabus of seven protocols. *Phi Delta Kappan, 91*(4), 32–34.

Francis, D. J., Lesaux, N., Kieffer, M., & Rivera, H. (2006). *Research-based recommendations for instruction and academic interventions.* Houston: Texas Institute for Measurement, Evaluation, and Statistics.

Freeman, Y. S., Freeman, D. E., & Mecuri, S. (2002). *Closing the achievement gap: How to reach limited-formal schooling and long-term English learners.* Portsmouth, NH: Heinemann.

Freeman, Y. S., Freeman, D. E., & Mecuri, S. (2005). *Dual language essentials for teachers and administrators.* Portsmouth, NH: Heinemann.

Frey, N., & Fisher, D. (2006). *Language arts workshop: Purposeful reading and writing instruction.* Upper Saddle River, NJ: Merrill Education.

Fry, R., & Gonzales, F. (2008). *One-in-five and growing fast: A profile of Hispanic public school students.* Washington, DC: Pew Hispanic Center. Accessed at http://pewhispanic.org /files/reports/92.pdf on March 11, 2011.

Gallavan, N. P. (2009). *Developing performance-based assessments: Grades K–5.* Thousand Oaks, CA: Corwin Press.

Gee, J. P. (2007). *Social linguistics and literacies: Ideology in discourses.* New York: Taylor & Francis.

Genesee, F., Lindholm-Leary, K., Saunders, W. M., & Christian, D. (Eds.). (2006). *Educating English language learners: A synthesis of research evidence.* Cambridge, England: Cambridge University Press.

Genesee, F., Paradis, J., & Crago, M. B. (2004). *Dual language development and disorders: A handbook on bilingualism and second language learning.* Baltimore: Paul H. Brookes.

Gibbons, P. (2006). Steps for planning an integrated program for ESL learners in mainstream classes. In P. McKay (Ed.), *Planning and teaching creatively within a required curriculum for school-age learners* (pp. 215–233). Alexandria, VA: Teachers of English to Speakers of Other Languages.

Glatthorn, A. A. (1998). *Performance assessment and standards-based curricula: The achievement cycle.* Larchmont, NY: Eye on Education.

Goldenberg, C., & Coleman, R. (2010). *Promoting academic achievement among English learners: A guide to the research.* Thousand Oaks, CA: Corwin Press.

Gottlieb, M. (in press). An overview of language standards for elementary and secondary education. In C. Coombe, S. Stoynoff, F. Davidson, & B. O'Sullivan (Eds.), *The Cambridge guide to language assessment.* Cambridge, England: Cambridge University Press.

Gottlieb, M. (1995). Nurturing student learning through portfolios. *TESOL Journal, 5*(1), 12–14.

Gottlieb, M. (1999). *The language proficiency handbook: A practitioner's guide to instructional assessment.* Springfield: Illinois State Board of Education.

Gottlieb, M. (2003). *Large-scale assessment of English language learners: Addressing educational accountability in K–12 settings* (Professional Paper #6). Alexandria, VA: Teachers of English to Speakers of Other Languages.

Gottlieb, M. (2004a). *WIDA consortium K–12 English language proficiency standards for English language learners: Frameworks for large-scale state and classroom assessment—Overview document.* Madison: State of Wisconsin.

Gottlieb, M. (2004b). How do we assess English language learners? In *On our way to English: Teacher's guide* (pp. T74–T75). Barrington, IL: Rigby.

Gottlieb, M. (2006). *Assessing English language learners: Bridges from language proficiency to academic achievement.* Thousand Oaks, CA: Corwin Press.

Gottlieb, M. (2007a). *ELL assessment kit: Teacher's manual.* Austin, TX: Harcourt Achieve.

Gottlieb, M. (2007b). The concept of validity in a standards-based world. *Perspectives, TESOL Arabia, 14*(3), 4–8.

Gottlieb, M. (2008). *Assessing English language learners: A multimedia kit for professional development.* Thousand Oaks, CA: Corwin Press.

Gottlieb, M. (2009, March). *The contribution of preK–12 standards to assessment and language education policy.* Paper presented at the annual conference of the American Association for Applied Linguistics, Denver, CO.

Gottlieb, M., & Boals, T. (2005). On the road to MECCA: Assessing content-based instruction within a standards framework. In D. Kaufman & J. Crandall (Eds.), *Content-based instruction in primary and secondary school settings* (pp. 145–161). Alexandria, VA: Teachers of English to Speakers of Other Languages.

Gottlieb, M., Cranley, E., & Oliver, A. (2007). *English language proficiency standards and resource guide, prekindergarten through grade 12.* Madison: Board of Regents of the University of Wisconsin System.

Gottlieb, M., & Hamayan, E. (2007). Assessing oral and written language proficiency: A guide for psychologists and teachers. In G. B. Esquivel, E. C. Lopez, & S. G. Nahari (Eds.), *Handbook of multicultural school psychology: An interdisciplinary perspective* (pp. 245–263). New York: Erlbaum.

Gottlieb, M., Katz, A., & Ernst-Slavit, G. (2009). *Paper to practice: Using the TESOL English language proficiency standards in preK–12.* Alexandria, VA: Teachers of English to Speakers of Other Languages.

Gottlieb, M., & Nguyen, D. (2007). *Assessment and accountability in language education programs: A guide for administrators and teachers.* Philadelphia: Caslon.

Gray, L., Thomas, N., Lewis, L., & Tice, P. (2010). *Educational technology in U.S. public schools: Fall 2008.* Washington, DC: U.S. Department of Education/Institute of Education Sciences/National Center for Education Statistics.

Gregory, G. H., & Kuzmich, L. (2004). *Data driven differentiation in the standards-based classroom.* Thousand Oaks, CA: Corwin Press.

Guskey, T. R., & Bailey, J. M. (2001). *Developing grading and reporting systems for student learning.* Thousand Oaks, CA: Corwin Press.

Hale, J. A. (2007). *A guide to curriculum mapping.* Thousand Oaks, CA: Corwin Press.

Halliday, M. A. K. (1976). *System and function in language.* London: Oxford University Press.

Hamayan, E., Marler, B., Sanchez-Lopez, C., & Damico, J. (2007). *Special education considerations for English language learners: Delivering a continuum of services.* Philadelphia: Caslon.

Hamayan, E., & Perlman, R. (1990). *Preparing mainstream classroom teachers to teach potentially proficient English students.* Washington, DC: National Clearinghouse for Bilingual Education.

Harry, B., & Klingner, J. (2006). *Why are so many minority students in special education?* New York: Teachers College Press.

Harry, B., & Klingner, J. (2007). Discarding the deficit model: Improving instruction for students with learning needs. *Educational Leadership, 64*(5), 16–21.

Hein, G. E., & Price, S. (1994). *Active assessment for active science: A guide for elementary school teachers.* Portsmouth, NH: Heinemann.

Hernandez, D. J. (2010). A demographic portrait of young English language learners. In E. E. García & E. C. Frede (Eds.), *Young English language learners: Current research and emerging directions for practice and policy* (pp. 10–41). New York: Teachers College Press.

Hopstock, P. J., & Stephenson, T. G. (2003). *Descriptive study of services to LEP students and LEP students with disabilities: Special topic report #2—Analysis of Office for Civil Rights data related to LEP students.* Washington, DC: U.S. Department of Education/ Office of English Language Acquisition.

Hord, S. M. (1997). Professional learning teams: What are they and why are they important? *Issues About Change, 6*(1). Accessed at www.sedl.org/pubs/catalog/items /cha35.html on March 11, 2011.

Horwitz, A. R., Uro, G., Price-Baugh, R., Simon, C., Uzzell, R., Lewis, S. et al. (2009). *Succeeding with English language learners: Lessons from the great city schools.* Washington, DC: Council of the Great City Schools.

Howard, E. R., Sugarman, J., & Christian, D. (2003). *Trends in two-way immersion education: A review of the research.* Baltimore: Center for Research on the Education of Students Placed at Risk.

Howard, E. R., Sugarman, J., Christian, D., Lindholm-Leary, K. J., & Rogers, D. (2007). *Guiding principles for dual language education* (2nd ed.). Washington, DC: Center for Applied Linguistics.

Individuals with Disabilities Education Improvement Act of 2004, Pub. L. No. 108-466, 118 Stat. 2647, (2004).

Irujo, S. (Ed.). (2000). *Integrating the ESL standards into classroom practice: Grades 6–8.* Alexandria, VA: Teachers of English to Speakers of Other Languages.

Jacobs, H. H. (2004). *Getting results with curriculum mapping.* Alexandria, VA: Association for Supervision and Curriculum Development.

Kane, M. T. (1992). An argument-based approach to validity. *Psychological Bulletin, 112*(3), 527–535.

Katz, A. (in press). Linking assessment with instructional aims and learning. In C. Coombe, S. Stoynoff, F. Davidson, & B. O'Sullivan (Eds.), *The Cambridge guide to language assessment.* Cambridge, England: Cambridge University Press.

Kaufman, D., & Crandall, J. (Eds.). (2005). *Content-based instruction in primary and secondary school settings.* Alexandria, VA: Teachers of English to Speakers of Other Languages.

Kieffer, M. J., Lesaux, N., Rivera, M., & Frances, D. J. (2009). Accommodations for English language learners taking large-scale assessments: A meta-analysis on effectiveness and validity. *Review of Educational Research, 79*(3), 1168–1201.

Klingner, J. K., Hoover, J. J., & Baca, L. M. (2008). *Why do English language learners struggle with reading? Distinguishing language acquisition from learning disabilities.* Thousand Oaks, CA: Corwin Press.

Koch, R., & Schwartz-Petterson, J. (2000). *The portfolio guidebook: Implementing quality in an age of standards.* Norwood, MA: Christopher-Gordon.

LaCelle-Peterson, M., & Rivera, C. (1994). Is it real for all kids? A framework for equitable assessment policies for English language learners. *Harvard Education Review, 64*(1), 55–75.

Lachat, M. A. (2004). *Standards-based instruction and assessment for English language learners.* Thousand Oaks, CA: Corwin Press.

Lindholm-Leary, K. J. (2001). *Dual language education.* Clevedon, England: Multilingual Matters.

Lindholm-Leary, K. J., & Hargett, G. (2007). *Evaluator's toolkit for dual language programs.* Washington, DC: Center for Applied Linguistics. Accessed at www.cal.org/twi /EvalToolkit/index.htm on March 11, 2011.

Lindholm, K. J., & Molina, R. (2000). Two-way bilingual education: The power of two languages in promoting educational success. In J. V. Tinajero & R. A. DeVillar (Eds.), *The power of two languages 2000: Effective dual-language use across the curriculum* (pp. 163–174). New York: McGraw-Hill.

Linn, R. L., Baker, E. L., & Dunbar, S. B. (1991). Complex, performance-based assessment: Expectations and validation criteria. *Educational Researcher, 20*(8), 15–21.

Marzano, R. J. (2004). *Building background knowledge for academic achievement.* Alexandria, VA: Association for Supervision and Curriculum Development.

Marzano, R. J. (2006). *Classroom assessment and grading that work.* Alexandria, VA: Association for Supervision and Curriculum Development.

Marzano, R. J., & Kendall, J. S. (1996). *Designing standards-based districts, schools, and classrooms.* Aurora, CO: Mid-Continent Regional Educational Laboratory.

McKay, P. (2006). *Assessing young language learners.* Cambridge, England: Cambridge University Press.

McLaughlin, M. W., & Shephard, L. A. (1995). *Improving education through standards-based reform.* Stanford, CA: National Academy of Education.

Menken, K. (2008). *English learners left behind: Standardized testing as language policy.* Clevedon, England: Multilingual Matters.

Menken, K., & Kleyn, T. (2009). The difficult road for long-term English learners. *Educational Leadership, 66*(7). Accessed at www.ascd.org/publications/educational _leadership/apr09/v0166/num07/The_Difficult_RRoa_for_Long-Term_English _Learners.aspx on March 11, 2011.

Messick, S. (1988). The once and future issues of validity: Assessing the meaning and consequences of measurement. In H. Wainer & H. Braun (Eds.), *Test validity* (pp. 33–45). Hillsdale, NJ: Erlbaum.

Miramontes, O. B., Nadeau, A., & Commins, N. (1997). *Restructuring schools for linguistic diversity: Linking decision making to effective programs.* New York: Teachers College Press.

Mislevy, R. J., Steinberg, L. S., & Almond, R. G. (1999). *Evidence-centered assessment design.* Accessed at www.education.umd.edu/EDMS/mislevy/papers/ECD_overview .html on March 11, 2011.

Mohan, B. (1986). *Language and content.* Reading, MA: Addison-Wesley.

Moss, C. M., & Brookhart, S. M. (2009). *Advancing formative assessment in every classroom: A guide for instructional leaders.* Alexandria, VA: Association for Supervision and Curriculum Development.

National Clearinghouse for English Language Acquisition and Language Instruction Educational Programs. *The growing numbers of limited English proficient students, 1995/96–2005–06.* Washington, DC: Author. Accessed at www.ncela.gwu.edu/files /uploads/4/GrowingLEP_0506.pdf on March 11, 2011.

National Institute of Child Health and Human Development. (2000). *Report of the National Reading Panel: Teaching children to read—An evidence-based assessment of the scientific research literature on reading and its implications for reading instruction (NIH Publication No. 00–4769).* Washington, DC: Department of Health and Human Services.

No Child Left Behind Act of 2001, 20 U.S.C. § 6319 (2008).

Olsen, L. (2009). *Reparable harm: Fulfilling the unkept promise of educational opportunity for California's long term English learners.* Long Beach, CA: Californians Together.

O'Malley, J. M., & Pierce, L. V. (1996). *Authentic assessment for English language learners: Practical approaches for teachers.* New York: Addison-Wesley.

Payán, R. M., & Nettles, M. T. (2008). *Current state of English language learners in the U.S. K–12 student population.* Princeton, NJ: Educational Testing Service. Accessed at www.ets.org/Media/Conferences_and_Events/pdf/ELLsympsium/ELL_factsheet .pdf on July 2, 2011.

Popham, W. J. (2008). *Transformative assessment.* Alexandria, VA: Association for Supervision and Curriculum Development.

Popham, W. J. (2009). Data: Now what? *Educational Leadership, 66*(4), 85–86.

Ramsey, A., & O'Day, J. (2010). *Title III policy: State of the states (ESEA evaluation brief)— The English language acquisition, language enhancement, and Academic Achievement Act.* Washington, DC: American Institutes for Research.

Reeves, D. (2004). *Accountability for learning: How teachers and school leaders can take charge.* Alexandria, VA: Association for Supervision and Curriculum Development.

Rothenberg, C., & Fisher, D. (2007). *Teaching English language learners: A differentiated approach.* Upper Saddle River, NJ: Pearson Education.

Royer, J. M., & Carlo, M. S. (1991). Assessing the language acquisition progress of limited English proficient students: Problems and a new alternative. *Applied Measurement in Education, 4*(2), 85–113.

Rutherford, P. (2002). *Instruction for all students.* Alexandria, VA: Just ASK.

Scarcella, R. (2003). *Academic English: A conceptual framework* (Technical Report 2003–1). Irvine: University of California Linguistic Minority Research Institute.

Schleppegrell, M. J. (2004). *The language of schooling: A functional linguistics perspective.* Mahwah, NJ: Erlbaum.

Shohany, E. (2001). *The power of tests: A critical perspective on the uses of language tests.* Essex, England: Pearson.

Short, D. (1996). *Integrating language and culture in the social studies: Teacher training packet.* Washington, DC: Center for Applied Linguistics.

Short, D. (2010, March). *Findings from the 2008-09 newcomer program database.* Presented at the 44th annual convention of the Teachers of English to Speakers of Other Languages, Boston, MA.

Smallwood, B. A. (Ed.). (2000). *Integrating the ESL standards into classroom practice: Grades preK–2.* Alexandria, VA: Teachers of English to Speakers of Other Languages.

Snow, M. A. (Ed.). (2000). *Implementing the ESL standards for pre-K–12 students through teacher education.* Alexandria, VA: Teachers of English to Speakers of Other Languages.

Spolsky, B. (1989). *Conditions for second language learning.* Oxford, England: Oxford University Press.

Stiggins, R. (2008). *Assessment manifesto: A call for the development of balanced assessment systems.* Portland, OR: Educational Testing Service.

Stiggins, R. J. (2005). *Student-involved assessment FOR learning* (4th ed.). Columbus, OH: Merrill Prentice Hall.

Stiggins, R. J., Arter, J., Chappuis, J., & Chappuis, S. (2006). *Classroom assessment for student learning: Doing it right, using it well.* Portland, OR: Educational Testing Service.

Supovitz, J. A. (2002). Developing communities of instructional practice. *Teachers College Board, 104*(8), 1591–1626.

Tabors, P. O. (2008). *One child, two languages* (2nd ed.). Baltimore: Paul H. Brookes.

Teachers of English to Speakers of Other Languages. (1998). *Managing the assessment process: A framework for measuring student attainment of the ESL standards* (TESOL Professional Paper #5). Alexandria, VA: Author.

Teachers of English to Speakers of Other Languages. (2001). *Scenarios for ESL standards-based assessment.* Alexandria, VA: Author.

Teachers of English to Speakers of Other Languages. (2006). *PreK–12 English language proficiency standards.* Alexandria, VA: Author.

Thompson, S., & Thurlow, M. (2002). *Universally designed assessments: Better tests for everyone! NCEO policy directions.* Minneapolis, MN: National Center on Educational Outcomes. Accessed at http://education.umn.edu/NCEO/OnlinePubs/Policy13.htm on March 11, 2011.

Tomlinson, C. A. (1999). *The differentiated classroom: Responding to the needs of all learners.* Alexandria, VA: Association for Supervision and Curriculum Development.

Tomlinson, C. A. (2004). *How to differentiate instruction in mixed-ability classrooms* (2nd ed.). Alexandria, VA: Association for Supervision and Curriculum Development.

Trumbull, E., & Farr, B. (Eds.). (2000). *Grading and reporting student progress in an age of standards.* Norwood, MA: Christopher-Gordon.

Valdes, G. (2005). Bilingualism, heritage language learners, and SLA research: Opportunities lost or seized? *Modern Language Journal, 89*(3), 410–426.

Vaughn, S., & Ortiz, A. (2008). *Response to intervention in reading for English language learners.* Washington, DC: RTI Action Network. Accessed at www.rtinetwork.org /Learn/Diversity/ar/EnglishLanguage on March 11, 2011.

Vygotsky, L. (1962). *Thought and language.* Cambridge, MA: MIT Press.

Weir, C. J. (2005). *Language testing and validation: An evidence-based approach.* Basingstoke, Hampshire, England: Palgrave Macmillan.

WIDA Consortium. (2007). *English language proficiency standards and resource guide prekindergarten through grade 12* (4th ed.). Madison, WI: Board of Regents of the University of Wisconsin System.

Wolf, M. K., Herman, J. L., & Dietel, R. (2010). *Improving the validity of English language learner assessment systems* (Policy Brief 10). Los Angeles: National Center for Research on Evaluation, Standards, and Student Testing.

Wright, W. E. (2007). A catch-22 for language learners. *Educational Leadership, 64,* 22–27.

Zwiers, J. (2008). *Building academic language: Essential practices for content classrooms, grades 5–12.* San Francisco: Jossey-Bass.

Index

Common Formative Assessment
Kim Bailey and Chris Jakicic
The catalyst for real student improvement begins with a decision to implement common formative assessments. In this conversational guide, the authors offer tools, templates, and protocols to incorporate common formative assessments into the practices of a PLC to monitor and enhance student learning.
BKF538

Implementing RTI With English Learners
Douglas Fisher, Nancy Frey, and Carol Rothenberg
Learn why RTI is the ideal framework for supporting English learners. Follow the application and effectiveness of RTI through classroom examples and the stories of four representative students of varying ages, nationalities, and language proficiency levels.
BKF397

Teaching Reading & Comprehension to English Learners, K–5
Margarita Calderón
Raise achievement for English learners through new instructional strategies and assessment processes. This book addresses the language, literacy, and content instructional needs of ELs and frames quality instruction within effective schooling structures and the implementation of RTI.
BKF402

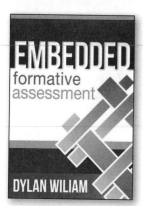

Embedded Formative Assessment
Dylan Wiliam
Emphasizing the instructional side of formative assessment, this book explores in-depth the use of classroom questioning, learning intentions and success criteria, feedback, collaborative and cooperative learning, and self-regulated learning to engineer effective learning environments for students.
BKF418

Solution Tree | Press

a division of

Solution Tree

Visit solution-tree.com or call 800.733.6786 to order.